Complete Vocal Fitness

Complete Vocal Fitness

*A Singer's Guide to Physical Training,
Anatomy, and Biomechanics*

Claudia Friedlander

ROWMAN & LITTLEFIELD
Lanham • Boulder • New York • London

Published by Rowman & Littlefield
An imprint of The Rowman & Littlefield Publishing Group, Inc.
4501 Forbes Boulevard, Suite 200, Lanham, Maryland 20706
www.rowman.com

Unit A, Whitacre Mews, 26-34 Stannary Street, London SE11 4AB

British Library Cataloguing in Publication Information Available

Library of Congress Cataloging-in-Publication Data
Name: Friedlander, Claudia, 1964–, author.
Title: Complete vocal fitness : a singer's guide to physical training, anatomy, and biomechanics / Claudia Friedlander.
Description: Lanham : Rowman & Littlefield, 2018.
Identifiers: LCCN 2018005948 (print) | LCCN 2018007135 (ebook) | ISBN 9781538105450 (ebook) | ISBN 9781538105436 (cloth : alk. paper) | ISBN 9781538105443 (pbk. : alk. paper)
Subjects: LCSH: Singing—Physiological aspects. | Singing—Instruction and study.
Classification: LCC MT821 (ebook) | LCC MT821 .F75 2018 (print) | DDC 783/.043—dc23
LC record available at https://lccn.loc.gov/2018005948

∞™ The paper used in this publication meets the minimum requirements of American National Standard for Information Sciences—Permanence of Paper for Printed Library Materials, ANSI/NISO Z39.48-1992.

Printed in the United States of America

Contents

Preface

For as long as I can remember, I have always loved to sing.

Growing up, however, I did not possess a voice that others considered beautiful. Years of fruitless auditions for middle and high school musical theater productions finally led me to give up singing in favor of playing the clarinet, which earned me far more encouragement and success.

Then, shortly after completing my bachelor's in music as a clarinetist, something extraordinary happened. I engaged in a course of bioenergetic analysis, a therapeutic form of bodywork designed to resolve chronic muscular tensions and improve breathing. These sessions exposed long-ingrained habitual patterns of holding that were inhibiting not only my breathing but also movement throughout my throat, mouth, and face. As I became capable of releasing these tensions, my voice gradually became notably more resonant and my range much easier to navigate. I took up singing again for the first time in years . . . and when I finally found the courage to perform in public, people began to tell me that they found my voice beautiful.

The discovery that such a profound change could take place in my voice brought me tremendous joy. It also inspired me to question other long-held assumptions about my body's limitations, such as an apparent lack of athletic aptitude.

As a child I was even less a natural athlete than I was a natural singer. Throughout my adolescence I was bullied for being weak and uncoordinated. I recall how humiliating it was in middle school to have to perform a gymnastics floor routine in front of my peers when I could barely execute a decent somersault, to be picked last for the basketball team, and to be eliminated in the first round of track-and-field meets.

I began to wonder: If I could learn to free my voice, couldn't I *also* learn to free my body? While browsing in a bookstore, I came across *A Woman's Book of Strength* by Karen Andes. This was in the early 1990s. Andes had earned some fame as Cher's trainer, and she capitalized on it to reach out to and empower women like me who longed for physical strength but had no idea where to begin. Her book helped me discover that while I might not have had an aptitude for gymnastics or basketball, I had quite an aptitude for strength training. I have worked out consistently ever since.

This is how I came to identify as both a singer and an athlete. These experiences also kindled my desire to teach. I was so grateful to find myself enjoying these newfound abilities that I had feared would remain forever beyond my grasp. I figured that if *I* could learn to do these things despite early setbacks and discouragement, perhaps I could help others to learn to do them too.

My graduate studies in voice performance were thus informed by my experiences as an instrumentalist and an athlete, as well as a keen interest in pedagogy. It was the first time I had ever studied alongside so many serious classical singers, and I shared with them my story about how bodywork had freed up my throat and articulators. Shortly after that conversation, my voice teacher summoned me to her studio for a chat. "It has come to my attention that you have been participating in primal scream therapy," she announced. "I feel that it is my responsibility to inform you that I do not approve." While I recovered from my amazement at how quickly gossip can ricochet around voice departments, I attempted to assure her that there was no primal screaming (whatever that is) going on and to explain my experiences. She maintained that such practices had no place in her studio and informed me that if I insisted on continuing down this path that I would have to find a new teacher.

In the years that followed I discovered that she was far from alone in expressing reservations about the potential impact of bodywork or other physical activities on the voice. Subtle practices like the Alexander Technique and relaxation methods were deemed useful and safe, but anything that had the potential to create structural changes in the singer's instrument was regarded with suspicion: The miraculous voice you were born with must never be tampered with.

Of course, I knew firsthand that I would not be singing *at all* had my own voice not undergone significant positive structural changes. While I imagined that not all singers were burdened with chronic muscular tensions to the extent that I had been, it seemed likely that many would benefit from a means of exposing and alleviating any problematic tensions that affected their voices.

When I began teaching voice full-time myself, it became clear to me that many of my students were indeed being held back in their ability to apply the technical principles I shared with them. I could see that chronic tensions and postural distortions often kept them from being able to move their bodies and voices in the direction I asked them to. I knew that these tensions and imbalances could be resolved, so I refused to accept them as built-in limitations of my students' instruments. But the means available to me in the voice studio were insufficient. I had to find a solution.

Tensions are muscular contractions. Postural distortions are the result of muscular imbalances. I wondered whether conditioning the skeletomuscular system itself could evoke positive structural changes that would give singers the mobility necessary to cultivate optimal breath and laryngeal coordination, as well as the physical stability to maintain excellent singing technique while meeting the demands of stage movement.

I began to observe the trainers at my gym. I noted strong similarities between the way they instructed their clients and the way I worked in the voice studio, and I thought, "I can do this!" I signed up for a fitness certification course and applied for a job. The manager naturally wanted to know why a woman in her late thirties with a doctorate and no fitness experience was seeking an entry-level position at his gym. I explained, "I'm tired of telling my voice students to stand up straight and take a deep breath. It doesn't work. I need a way to help them actually *do* it."

I worked in gyms for two years. My clients ranged in age from their early twenties to mid seventies, and they represented a broad range of strengths, dysfunctions, aspirations, and learning styles. And while I *did* learn how to help my students become capable of standing up straight and taking a deep breath, the experience ended up being far more valuable than I ever could have imagined. The deep understanding of biomechanics and motor learning that I acquired in the gym has become integral to my pedagogical approach in the studio.

The concept of fitness training for singers was a hard sell at first. As I pointed out in "Sport-Specific Training for the Vocal Athlete," my 2005 article for *Classical Singer Magazine*:

> Generations of voice professionals have warned singers against vigorous exercise. P. Mario Marafioti, Enrico Caruso's laryngologist, wrote that "While it is urgent for a boxer or a fencer to keep his muscles in continual training, it is hardly necessary for a thinker, a writer, or anybody who is devoted to a purely intellectual form of activity to overtax his physical strength. As singing belongs to this latter class of activities, all books and methods advocating physical training for singers seem to consider singing more as a muscular action than as an intellectual achievement. . . . We would suggest that singers take care of their health just by following the normal rules of all intelligent people, without exerting themselves in any form of physical training." Richard Miller assents to athletic activities that "ensure excellent, general physical condition and if they are not strenuously carried out past the age when physical exercise should be cut back," but comments that "Even in the prime years, it is questionable that muscular development, including those muscles directly related to singing, need attain special dimensions for singing." Barbara Doscher and Meribeth Bunch agree that light forms of exercise, particularly swimming, are beneficial, but heavy weight lifting should be discouraged. Pedagogy books typically include an entire chapter on the singer's formant but devote a mere paragraph to exercise, and the tone is usually cautionary.

In the years since my article first appeared, I have been delighted to witness an ever-increasing interest in and enthusiasm for fitness among the singer community. Since 2007, the *Barihunks Blog* has celebrated the athletic achievements of low-voiced men on and off the operatic stage. In 2013, *Classical Singer* invited me to initiate a monthly column on fitness and singing called "Musings on Mechanics." Stability balls and resistance bands are now frequently seen in voice studios. And in June 2018 (right around the date of this book's publication), the Voice Foundation will devote the Friday-morning special session of their annual symposium to presentations on exercise and the voice. But for me, of course, the most gratifying evidence that this is an idea whose time has finally arrived is the fact that you are now reading this book!

The instrument that you were born with is indeed a miraculous thing. Its miraculous nature stems from its extraordinary malleability and responsiveness to training. Through achieving balanced strength and flexibility, you can unlock its full potential.

Acknowledgments

I am indebted to an extraordinarily diverse group of people and organizations for the inspiration and support to write this book.

W. Stephen Smith, my dear friend and mentor, taught me that anything can be made manageable when broken down into simple components. Mark Milani, my first fitness trainer, showed me that I was capable of becoming far stronger than I ever imagined possible. Artist Michael T. Fry put a copy of *The Anatomy Coloring Book* in my hands and persuaded me that, with patience, this was a topic I could master.

I am grateful to the National Academy of Sports Medicine for the exceptional training and technologies they provide to fitness professionals and for their ongoing commitment to cutting-edge sports science research. Particular thanks go to Stacey Cooke Penney, for encouraging my interdisciplinary writing about fitness, and singing and Rick Richey, who was also my fitness manager when I first became a personal trainer.

David Ley and Elissa Weinzimmer, creators of Vibrant Voice Technique, have pioneered methods to optimize singers' physical instruments that have proved invaluable for my work in both the studio and the gym.

Karen Andes, Blandine Calais-Germaine, Barbara Doscher, and Meribeth Dayme wrote books that were vital not only for my education but also for the inspiration to write my own.

Sara Thomas, editor of *Classical Singer* magazine, offered me a platform for writing about singing and fitness in the form of my monthly "Musings on Mechanics" column; years earlier her predecessor, Carla Wood, launched my writing career by encouraging me to write an article on the topic.

Natalie Mandziuk and the editorial staff at Rowman & Littlefield have sustained me with their belief in and invaluable assistance with this project. Rowman publishes many of the titles that formed my foundational understanding of vocal pedagogy, and I am so honored to count myself among their authors.

The National Association of Teachers of Singing, the Voice Foundation, Opera America, and the Performing Arts Medicine Association all helped me find my voice and connect with the wider musical community through their invitations to present at their symposia and serve on discussion panels.

William Holt and his wonderful staff at Hype Gym provided a bright and versatile environment for our photo shoot.

Bioenergeticists Judith and Michael Jamieson gave me greater access to my own body; Alexander Technique teachers Lori Schiff and Malcolm Balk helped me to reeducate it.

I am grateful to Melissa Malde for her excellent application of body mapping principles for articulation anatomy; Matthew Hoch and Mary J. Sandage for adapting exercise science principles for vocal warm-up techniques; Nicholas Pallesen for sharing his hypnosis expertise with the classical vocal community; and David Salsbery Fry, whose personal experiences navigating the treacherous waters of the American healthcare system formed the foundation of my chapter on maintaining robust health while pursuing a performance career.

The sensational artwork in this book would not have been possible without the generosity of the nearly 300 patrons who pledged my Kickstarter campaign, especially major contributors Judith Friedlander and Jamie Patterson, two of the most dedicated avocational singers a voice teacher could ask for.

The *Barihunks*, *Sybaritic Singer*, and *OperAthletic* blogs shine a spotlight on the athletic nature of classical singing, helping to lay to rest the archetype of the ungainly opera singer.

My delightfully irreverent social media community is a daily source of support and inspiration, most notably the NEW New Forum for Classical Singers, the Professional Voice Teachers, the Collective Union to Nurture Talent and Singing, and the Danger Clams Fitness Fun Club Facebook groups.

The countless voice students and fitness clients I have been privileged to teach over the years provide a vibrant laboratory of sound and movement that continually shapes my understanding.

A heartfelt thanks to my friends outside the classical singing and fitness communities for keeping my perspective broad and my life in balance.

Finally, I could never have undertaken this project without the unflagging encouragement of my beloved husband, mother, and sister. Their steadfast belief in my vision has sustained me through the challenges and self-doubts that inevitably attend a project of this scope, and I feel so fortunate to have had their support.

Introduction

Sport-Specific Training for the Vocal Athlete

What does the body of an Olympic diver have in common with a Stradivarius violin?

They are state-of-the-art examples of form following function.

Divers spend roughly half their training time in the water. The other half is devoted to flexibility, weight training, and gymnastic and cardiorespiratory exercises. They perform stretches that maximize range of motion for all midair movements. They follow a weight-training regimen designed to build strength in their legs, core, and shoulders and to minimize muscular bulk in their chest and back that would make them less aerodynamic. They practice somersaults and flips on a mat and jump on a trampoline in order to execute a greater number of repetitions for these movements than would be possible on a diving board. They engage in a vigorous cardiorespiratory program so they can climb long flights of stairs to the diving board without depleting the energy they will need for the dive itself. This regimen confers the explosive leg power to achieve optimal height when they launch, the core strength and stability to execute swift, well-controlled flips and inversions, and the shoulder strength to gracefully absorb the shock of impact when they hit the water. Their lean, streamlined, sculpted physiques are the result of their commitment to excellence in their sport.

Like all fine instruments, Stradivarius violins were crafted for enduring playability and beauty of sound. Antonio Stradivari's structural design yielded so reliable a level of stability that his surviving specimens remain in robust use despite having been played by the world's most demanding musicians for more than 300 years. The skill with which he selected and conditioned his wood and the precision with which he shaped it yielded instruments of extraordinary resonance whose sonic qualities have continued to evolve over generations. Throughout his career, Stradivari experimented with the materials and dimensions he used to construct his instruments, always seeking to improve upon his own design. His achievements continue to wield a strong influence on modern luthiers. Advances in technology and acoustical science may someday yield instruments considered superior to Stradivari's, but the criteria for a state-of-the-art violin remain as they were in his day. The value of a violin lies in its endurable playability and its beauty of sound. Its form is a testament to the excellence of its function.

The tools that enable athletes to achieve elite status and the principles espoused by master instrument builders hold immense value for singers wishing to optimize their bodies for performance. This book will show you how to apply tenets of sport-specific training and instrument design to your own vocal instrument so that your expressive impulses can flow through it effortlessly, your technique unimpeded by tensions and imbalances.

Sport-Specific Training

Sport-specific training refers to exercise regimens designed to help athletes achieve peak performance. You might get better at your sport just by playing it, but coaches and trainers know that conditioning the muscles and drilling the movements required for your sport will accelerate your improvement and optimize your performance.

Imagine that you play third base for a baseball team. Your job often involves throwing the ball long distances with speed and precision. This requires the ability to generate tremendous explosive force with your pectoral, anterior deltoid, and triceps muscles while stabilizing your shoulder, as well as generating rotational power and momentum through your legs and torso while stabilizing this movement with the muscles in your lumbo-pelvic-hip complex.

Your sport-specific training regimen might include a dumbbell chest press to strengthen your chest and triceps, a sequence of movements to stabilize your rotator cuffs, squats to build power in your legs, and a Pilates routine to stabilize your core.

Your strength training sessions would take place in a gym using tools like free weights and cables.

For cultivating peak performance, it is equally important that you spend time in the field with a ball, a glove, and your teammates, practicing the actual movements and activities you will perform in an actual game: fielding, throwing, and catching the ball. Your training regimen includes repeating these movements over and over again, with a view to improving your reflexes, hand-eye coordination, and collaborative synergy with teammates. Sport-specific training can be broken down into two categories:

- Quality of force production and stability are cultivated in the gym

- Coordination, skill, and teamwork are developed in the field

To design a sport-specific training program for any athletic endeavor, you must analyze the skills involved and identify the type and degree of force production and stabilization required for each. You must also determine which of these skills are most effectively cultivated in the gym and which in the field.

When I compare traditional vocal education with the paradigm of sport-specific training, I find that singers' regimens focus almost exclusively on movements best trained in "the field"—the practice room and concert hall—with little time and consideration devoted to cultivating the types of physical force production and stability that would greatly enhance key components of their performance: alignment, stamina, and stabilization.

Alignment

Good alignment is essential for vocal development and performance. The spine provides the foundation from which all movement originates, and a well-aligned spine facilitates free laryngeal movement; full resonance; and expansive, coordinated breathing. Conversely, the common postural distortions that most people develop in the course of day-to-day living can significantly limit vocal function.

A sport-specific training program of any kind begins with a robust alignment assessment to identify postural imbalances and a program designed to correct them. To this end, sports scientists have designed movement screens that are easily applicable to vocal athletes. Improvements in alignment have been shown to shave crucial seconds off a 100-meter sprint or add vital length to a long jump; I will show how attaining optimal alignment can confer similar benefits for a singer's range, resonance, and breathing.

Stamina

An athlete's stamina can be measured by his or her ability to access stores of energy and regulate its expenditure. This ability is largely determined by how well the athlete is able to metabolize oxygen. The respiratory system's primary responsibility is distributing oxygen throughout the body, providing the vocal athlete with the energy needed not only for stage movement and singing but also for all essential survival needs moment to moment—circulation, digestion, cognition, and so on. Singing places further demands on the respiratory system because in addition to providing the medium for oxygen delivery, the breath must also serve as a sophisticated generator of sound.

Good cardiorespiratory fitness is therefore essential for singing. It provides the stamina crucial for sustaining long phrases and remaining energized throughout performances of two hours or more. The better your stamina, the better you'll be able to access the best of your technique regardless of the staging challenges your director creates for you, and the more options you will have for pacing and sustaining phrases and cadenzas. A sport-specific training program for any activity requiring stamina must include a cardiorespiratory regimen designed to improve oxygen consumption.

Stabilization

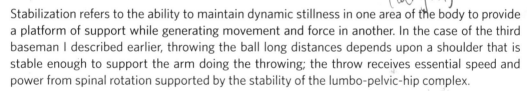

(larynx)

Stabilization refers to the ability to maintain dynamic stillness in one area of the body to provide a platform of support while generating movement and force in another. In the case of the third baseman I described earlier, throwing the ball long distances depends upon a shoulder that is stable enough to support the arm doing the throwing; the throw receives essential speed and power from spinal rotation supported by the stability of the lumbo-pelvic-hip complex.

Vocal athletes require stability to accomplish two distinct but related tasks: breath management and stage movement. The complex internal movements needed to generate optimal subglottal breath pressure while keeping the larynx disentangled require an ability to stabilize muscles in and around the core, shoulders, and rib cage. The ability to engage in stage movement while singing requires the ability to stabilize the shoulders, core, and lumbo-pelvic-hip complex so that the internal movements of vocal technique proceed unaffected by external movements of the body. A singer's sport-specific training regimen should draw on the vast repertoire of techniques that sports scientists have devised to help athletes of all kinds cultivate the dynamic stability and balance they need to maximize power where it will best serve their performance.

Singers who engage in a sport-specific regimen can systematically optimize their alignment, stamina, and stability, providing their technique with a strong foundation of support. Singers who do not are the operatic equivalent of third basemen who only improve to the extent possible through training in the field and playing the game. Even those for whom this might prove adequate would seriously raise their game with regular sessions at the gym.

Instrument Design and Function

Every voice is unique because every singer is unique—a singular manifestation of body, mind, and personality; an irreproducible combination of genetics, history, and emotional and psychological evolution. Every singer has a unique story to tell and a unique instrument through which to express it.

The truth of this sometimes leads to the unfortunate assumption that some people are born with superb vocal instruments while others inhabit bodies that will never be suitable for music-making—that great singers are born that way rather than trained. There may exist inherent physical characteristics that confer advantages upon aspiring singers in the same sense that height can give basketball players a competitive edge, but to my knowledge they have yet to be subject to a scientific study, and I have doubts as to whether such an examination would yield anything conclusive.

Singers themselves may be unique, but skill at singing is built, not born. Many, if not most, of the anatomical features involved in singing are highly malleable. We can each cultivate for ourselves a state-of-the-art vocal instrument. In order to accomplish this, we must first understand how our instrument functions, analyze how specific features of our anatomy comprise its various facets, and investigate how each one can be improved.

Vocal Instrument Design and Function: An Objective Analysis

Musical instruments of all kinds share some common components:

- An overall structural design that supports each individual part and integrates them with one another

- A generator—an energy source that stimulates vibration

- A vibrator

- A resonator

A master instrument builder understands how each component best fulfills its primary role as well as how to coordinate each one seamlessly with all others.

Structural Design

The musculoskeletal system provides foundational support for every element of the voice, and the condition of the spine has a direct impact on breathing, phonation, resonance, and articulation. The structural design of the vocal instrument can be optimized via a sport-specific training regimen designed to cultivate balanced alignment.

Generator

Breath plays the role of generator for the vocal instrument. An effective generator provides for consistency, stamina, and variable intensity of sound production. Optimizing breathing for singing therefore means:

- Establishing adequate flexibility in the abdominal area and rib cage to draw a full inhalation and release it effortlessly

- Developing strength and coordination throughout the torso to optimize subglottal breath pressure

- Cultivating sufficient cardiorespiratory fitness to simultaneously supply oxygen to the body and airflow to the voice

Vibrator

The vocal folds, housed within the larynx, serve the role of vibrator for the vocal instrument. To function optimally, the vocal folds themselves must be flexible, responsive, and free from chronic tension. The structures that move the vocal folds to vary pitch and registration must provide for smooth coordination and access to the fullest possible range of motion.

Resonator

For the vocal instrument, the resonator comprises the entire supraglottal tract, a highly variable space capable of molding vocal vibration into a wide variety of tone colors; the articulators further shape this vibration into well-defined phonemes. Optimal resonance provides an ideal acoustic structure for vocal amplification and projection. This requires a pharynx free from unconscious tensions, as well as articulators that are capable of moving independently of one another.

Vocal Instrument Design and Function: A Subjective Experience

A strictly physiological and mechanical description of vocal anatomy and function likely bears little resemblance to the way most singers experience their voices. Singers all begin as self-taught. As children, we learn to sing in much the same way we learn most other things—through exploration and imitation. We may receive some instruction in musicianship, but we are unlikely to pursue voice lessons until after we reach puberty and our voices become more mature and stable. We rely on instinct for matching pitch, navigating our range, managing our breath, and modulating registration. Our concept of how singing works is necessarily grounded in the sensory and aural feedback we receive from our voices, rather than in an understanding of the anatomy and movement involved.

Because we enjoy little direct control over much of the anatomy involved in singing and receive little sensory feedback from many of the muscles governing respiration and phonation, the sensations we associate with singing provide an incomplete and often inconsistent picture of what our bodies are doing. The aural feedback we receive can be misleading because the way we perceive the sounds we make is very different from the way audiences perceive them. We hear our own voices primarily through bone conduction, which emphasizes the transmission of lower frequencies over higher and provides for a very different experience of resonance than that received by our listeners, who hear our voices primarily through air conduction. Our instinctive, subjective conceptualization of how our voices work, therefore, may have little in common with anatomical accuracy.

Generator

While singers are usually aware that the breath is responsible for generating the voice, they tend to assess their breathing in quantitative terms because they experience feedback they get from their bodies in terms of whether they have *enough* breath to sustain a given phrase or note. Effective breathing is therefore instinctively defined by the ability to take in an adequate volume of air and then budget it well for the duration of a phrase. The oft-repeated admonishment to "sing from the diaphragm," while intended to encourage the sense of abdominal expansion and control associated with full, well-supported breathing, is misleading, because the diaphragm is neither located in the abdomen nor active during singing. Singers are frequently surprised to learn that the diaphragm is the major muscle of *inhalation*, while singing takes place during *exhalation*. The engagement singers sense in the abdominal area is the result of the activity of the abdominal musculature rather than the diaphragm.

Vibrator and Resonator

Singers experience the vibration and resonance of their voices in myriad subjective ways. While the larynx, housed in the throat, is generally understood to be "the voice box," the sounds and sensations stemming from vocal vibration are usually felt and perceived elsewhere. Low notes may seem to rumble in the chest area, while high notes may elicit a buzzy sensation in the cheekbones or other regions of the skull. Some singers learn to associate a sense of pressure and effort in the throat with effective vocal production and gauge improvement in terms of their ability to increase and sustain this level of effort. Others may manage resonance by seeking to "place" the voice in a location in their chest or skull that feels well-suited to projecting a given pitch or vowel.

While such subjective sensory and aural feedback is a valuable source of information, this information is most useful when interpreted in terms of objective vocal anatomy and function. At times our instincts serve us beautifully, but at other times they can lead us astray. The sensation of throat pressure a singer may come to associate with the production of a powerful sound is more likely to indicate a counterproductive degree of tension. The buzzing sensations in the chest or face they associate with effective resonance can be elicited without actually achieving the desired resonance.

We all necessarily begin as self-taught singers, but mastering vocal technique requires that we associate our subjective experiences with objective anatomy and function.

When singers regard the state of their instruments as immutable, they are likely to experience their voices as having built-in limitations and never realize that barriers to their breathing or range could be due to imbalances in their bodies that can be addressed outside the studio. Nearly everyone develops postural distortions and muscular imbalances simply by sitting for long hours in classrooms or in front of a computer; engaging in repetitive asymmetrical activities like shooting pool, playing guitar, or skateboarding; or recovering from an injury that leads you to favor one leg over the other for an extended period of time. Your body is the sum total of your habits and experiences, and no one develops a perfectly balanced musculature without concerted effort. The minor distortions and imbalances that you develop might create no problem whatsoever for the average human, but when a singer fails to address them, the singer is playing a dysfunctional instrument. The dysfunction may manifest as only a slightly exaggerated spinal curvature or asymmetry, but it will likely limit the singing in one or more ways.

The best teacher in the world can only teach a singer how to play the instrument they bring to the studio.

- If a postural distortion of their cervical spine is limiting movement of the structures governing phonation and resonance, it will likely also limit the singer's ability to apply techniques designed to improve range, registration, and tone.

- If muscular imbalances in the singer's torso are impeding his or her ability to fully expand the rib cage, they are also impeding the singer's ability to learn breath management.

- If the singer has not developed adequate oxygen consumption, the singer will not be able to sustain long phrases on a single breath despite excellent breath coordination.

If the source of a singer's problem rests with alignment, it can only be resolved through improving alignment. The same is true for any physical habits or tensions entangling the breathing, phonation, resonance, or articulation. It is my aim to provide you with the means and confidence to cultivate an instrument that responds beautifully to the technical and expressive demands you place upon it.

Rather than being fully formed, genetically determined permanent structures, all components of the vocal instrument can be trained in ways that expand and improve their function. If you've ever experienced a vocal breakthrough that gave you access to a wider range or fuller resonance, you have experienced firsthand the truth of this assertion. The purpose of this book is not to supplant techniques that have been facilitating valuable progress for you in the voice studio but rather to provide a biomechanical context for understanding how those techniques work while encouraging a more comprehensive approach to optimizing your instrument.

Clarinetists understand that fingering activates keys that, by means of springs, cover up holes with padded disks. The springs sometimes break; the pads age and need to be replaced from time to time. Clarinetists need to know how their instrument works so they can keep it in good working order. They also need to know whether a problem they've encountered is the result of faulty technique or a faulty instrument. Singers must cultivate similar relationships with their instruments.

How to Use This Book

This book was conceived as a user manual for your vocal instrument. It contains chapters covering the function, care, and optimization of your anatomy as they relate to singing. If you're the sort of person who reads the manual start-to-finish upon acquiring a new gadget, then I invite you to dive right in! If you picked up this volume in order to troubleshoot an issue that you are having with one component of your instrument or another or because you're interested in adapting an existing workout regimen to better meet your vocal needs, feel free to take a more targeted approach.

Chapters 1–4 combine an athletic training paradigm with an instrument-building paradigm to help you understand the biomechanics of the components of your instrument and assess their functions in order to optimize them individually and coordinate them together.

Chapter 5 delves into the mind/body connection essential for vocal artistry. In singing, the roles of musician and instrument are inseparably integrated; rather than manipulate an external object, the singer evokes music through fine neuromuscular control of the body. This chapter explores a variety of methods for both integrating mind and body and strengthening kinesthetic awareness.

Chapter 6 lays out a comprehensive sport-specific fitness training regimen for singers to optimize alignment, stamina, and balance. Completing the assessment screens outlined in chapter 1 will enable you to customize a program to meet your specific needs. It's wise to obtain medical clearance prior to embarking on a new fitness regimen, so be sure to consult your doctor, physical therapist, or other qualified health professional and incorporate any suggestions they may have into your routine.

Chapter 7 helps you design a warm-up routine that readies not just the vocal mechanism but also your whole body and mind to prime yourself for performance—vocally, physically, and psychologically.

Chapter 8 provides essential nutrition guidelines to support your exercise regimen, fuel performances, and maintain a high level of energy when faced with challenging travel and rehearsal schedules.

Chapter 9 offers strategies to support the overall health of your instrument, minimize the impact of common ailments, and secure appropriate and timely interventions when necessary. It also offers recommendations for protecting your voice when undergoing unrelated medical treatments or procedures.

Chapter 10 demonstrates that a singer who follows a health and fitness regimen designed to optimize the body for singing will naturally exude physical grace, power, balance, and beauty.

I wrote this book with a view to meeting the physical demands of acoustic classical singing, which requires the ability to project well in large spaces without the use of amplification. However, the concepts and exercises I present are equally beneficial for singers who specialize in musical theater and contemporary commercial styles. Nonclassical singers have been traditionally more likely to engage in vigorous fitness regimens, given the emphasis on dance skills and aesthetic standards for their performance genres. The fitness guidelines I recommend will help ensure that your exercise regimen prioritizes peak performance in singing while you pursue dance training, aesthetic outcomes, or any other fitness goals. I invite singers of all stripes to use this manual in any way that will raise your game as a vocal athlete.

1

Alignment

As a doctoral student, I devoured every book on vocal pedagogy I could get my hands on. However contrasting their approaches were for cultivating skill in breathing, vocal production, and articulation, they all emphasized good alignment as foundational for the development of technique. Some offered extensive physiological descriptions of the healthy spine and others detailed illustrations, but none offered much advice for achieving this crucial aspect of the singer's instrument. These texts left me with the impression that in order to sing well, I should hold myself in a way that would meet their descriptions and resemble their illustrations.

The concept of an ideal spinal position for singing makes sense when you relate vocal anatomy to musical instruments, nearly all of which are built around a stable base that supports moving parts and vibrating structures. Wind and brass instruments consist of tubes to which valves, rings, pads, and fingers can be appended to vary pitch, and stringed instruments are equipped with wooden necks that serve as stable structures to which strings can be affixed. For singers, the spine is the foundational structure that supports all of the moving parts that facilitate breathing, as well as activities of the larynx, articulators, and resonators. Unlike the stable structures that form the bodies of other instruments, however, our spines are extraordinarily mobile. Even in repose, our vertebrae remain in continual flux by virtue of their participation in the movements of respiration.

Alignment is inherently dynamic and therefore cannot be defined as an ideal position for singers to emulate. What our vocal instruments require are spines free of postural distortions, dynamically stabilized rather than rigidly held, so that we can activate the internal moving parts and vibrating structures that contribute to singing while remaining externally free to dramatically embody our roles.

Whether engaged in highly active operatic staging or the relative stillness of recital, singers must continually restabilize their bodies to support the mechanics of breath management, laryngeal activity, and articulation while accommodating movements of the limbs. The ability to stabilize not only the spine but also the core and major joints is essential for integrating the internal activities of singing with the demands of external movement.

While my later chapters focusing on anatomy are sport-specific to singing, the imperative to cultivate a well-aligned, dynamically stable spine is something we share with athletes of all stripes. A stable spine supports the explosive arm movements needed to pitch or hit a baseball, the strokes and kicks that propel swimmers through the water, and the specialized breath management and laryngeal coordination that classical singers cultivate in order to fill an immense concert hall with our voices. We stand to benefit just as significantly as other athletes do from the techniques developed over decades of sports science research for assessing and optimizing alignment.

Optimal Alignment

The spinal column, shown in figure 1.1, consists of twenty-four vertebrae, the sacrum, and the coccyx. The top seven vertebrae comprise the cervical spine; the middle twenty-three comprise the thoracic spine; the lower five comprise the lumbar spine. A healthy spine has three natural curves when viewed from the side (see figure 1.1).

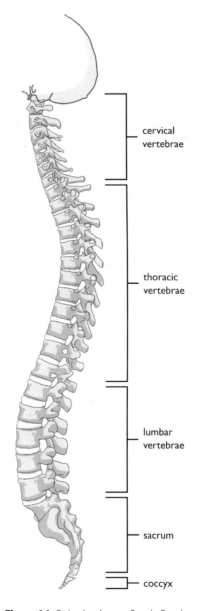

cervical
vertebrae

thoracic
vertebrae

lumbar
vertebrae

sacrum

coccyx

Figure 1.1 Spinal column. *Sandy Escobar.*

An anterior curve of the neck, or cervical spine. The cervical spine impacts range of motion for your larynx and articulators as well as the size, malleability, and integrity of your resonating cavities.

A posterior curve of the upper torso, or thoracic spine. The thoracic spine governs range of motion for your ribs and diaphragm and therefore influences both lung capacity and breath management.

An anterior curve of the lower back, or lumbar spine. The lumbar spine also impacts breathing, as the crura of the diaphragm originate in the lumbar vertebrae. It also supports your core and lumbo-pelvic-hip complex and is therefore vital for stabilizing movement as well as breathing.

Rather than stacking in a straight line, our vertebrae have evolved into this curved arrangement, each cushioned by intervertebral disks, in order to absorb the shock of various forces that impact our bodies. When faulty movement or sedentary habits cause these curves to become either exaggerated or straightened out, our internal and external mobility are compromised and our ability to neutralize shock is impeded.

Figure 1.2 represents a "neutral spine," the spinal column at rest, with all three curves in mutually supportive relationships with one another. A "neutral spine" or "ideal posture" is often described

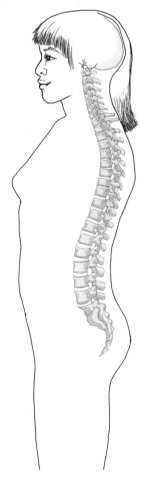

Figure 1.2 Neutral spine. *Sandy Escobar.*

as a position wherein a plumb line descending from the earlobe to the floor would pass through the tip of the shoulder, the high point of the pelvis, and the knee and would reach the floor just in front of the ankle.

Dr. Vladimir Janda's research in the late 1970s continues to serve as the foundation for the means many medical and fitness professionals use to assess and ameliorate the muscular imbalances responsible for postural problems. Janda identified three major distortion patterns.

In upper crossed syndrome, shown in figure 1.3, the head protrudes forward of the neck and the shoulders rotate in. In lower crossed syndrome, shown in figure 1.4, the pelvis tilts forward, exaggerating the curve of the lower back and usually also leading to exaggerated curves in the upper back and neck to compensate. In pronation distortion syndrome, shown in figure 1.5, the knees rotate internally and the feet turn out, impairing joint mechanics at the ankles, knees, and hips.

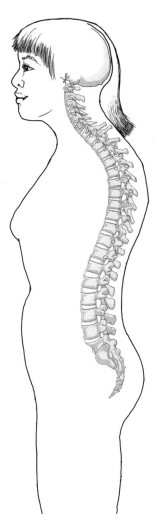

Figure 1.3 Upper crossed syndrome. *Sandy Escobar.*

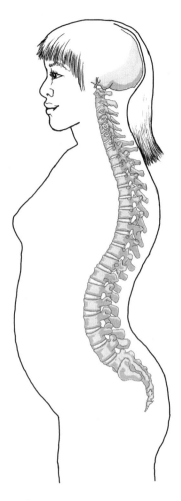

Figure 1.4 Lower crossed syndrome.
Sandy Escobar.

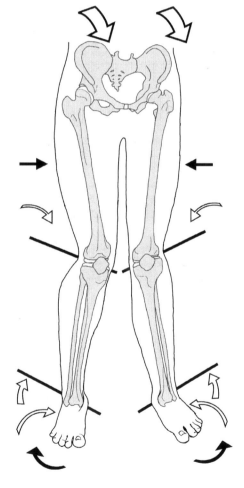

Figure 1.5 Pronation distortion syndrome.
Sandy Escobar.

If you consider the impact these three common distortion patterns can potentially have on vocal function, you'll understand how important it is for singers to be proactive about resolving them.

Upper Crossed Syndrome

Figure 1.6 shows healthy alignment supported by optimal length/tension relationships between the muscles of the upper torso and neck that support breathing and phonation. Figure 1.7 shows how the muscular imbalances characteristic of upper crossed syndrome distort alignment in this crucial area. The deep cervical flexors are weak and lengthened, unable to balance out tensions exerted on the neck by a tight upper trapezius and sternocleidomastoid. The rhomboids and middle/lower trapezius are weak and lengthened, allowing the shoulders to rotate internally, the sternum to collapse, and the muscles of the chest to become chronically tight. These conditions cause the head to protrude forward, restricting range of motion of the laryngeal cartilages at the cricothyroid joints; this limits overall range, particularly access to free high notes. The various strap muscles connecting the larynx to the sternum are shortened, which interferes with laryngeal stability. With the shoulders rounded in and sternum compressed, the ribs cannot fully expand, reducing lung capacity as well as strength and coordination in many of the muscles governing breath management.

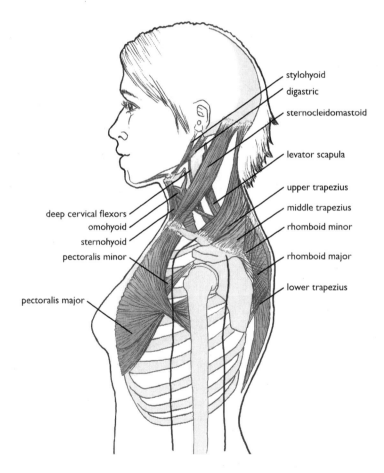

Figure 1.6 Good upper-body alignment facilitates healthy length/tension relationships between the muscles governing respiration, laryngeal function and articulation. *Sandy Escobar.*

Complete Vocal Fitness

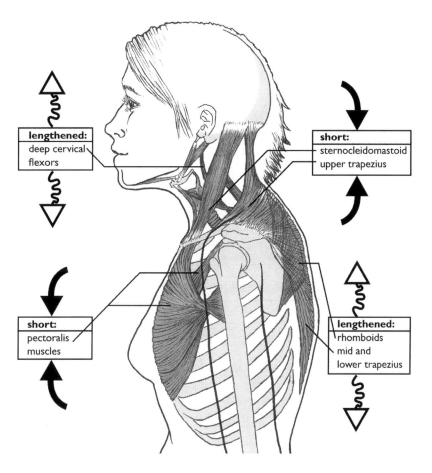

Figure 1.7 In upper crossed syndrome, tightness in the deep cervical flexors, upper trapezius and pectoral muscles pulls the head forward and compresses the sternum. *Sandy Escobar.*

Lower Crossed Syndrome

Figure 1.8 shows healthy alignment of the lower back and legs supported by optimal length/tension relationships throughout the musculature. Figure 1.9 shows how the muscular imbalances characteristic of lower crossed syndrome distort alignment of the lower ribs, lumbar spine and pelvis. Weakness in the abdominal muscles and tightness in the muscles of the lower back create an exaggerated curve of the lumbar spine, restricting range of motion for the lower ribs in the back; a compensatory tightness in the latissimus dorsi further impedes rib movement throughout the thoracic spine higher up. An exaggerated curve of the lower back also affects movement of the diaphragm, which is tethered by its crura to the lumbar vertebrae. Tightness in the hip flexors and weakness in the gluteal muscles cause the pelvis to tilt forward, creating a muscular imbalance throughout the core and compromising the strength and stability of the entire breath-support apparatus.

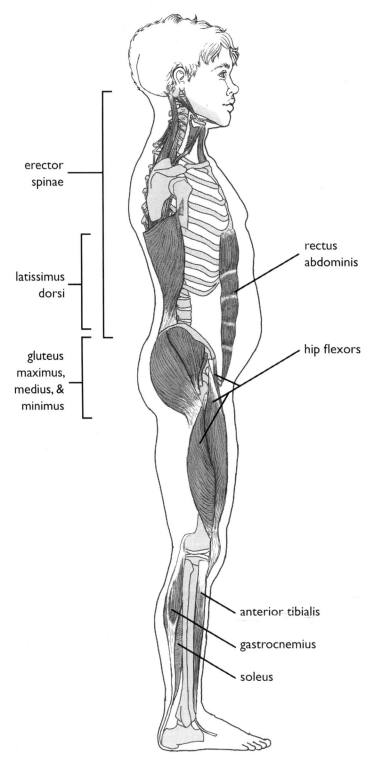

erector
spinae

latissimus
dorsi

gluteus
maximus,
medius, &
minimus

rectus
abdominis

hip flexors

anterior tibialis

gastrocnemius

soleus

Figure 1.8 Good lower-body alignment facilitates full range of motion for the diaphragm and ribs and provides for stability of the core. *Sandy Escobar.*

Complete Vocal Fitness

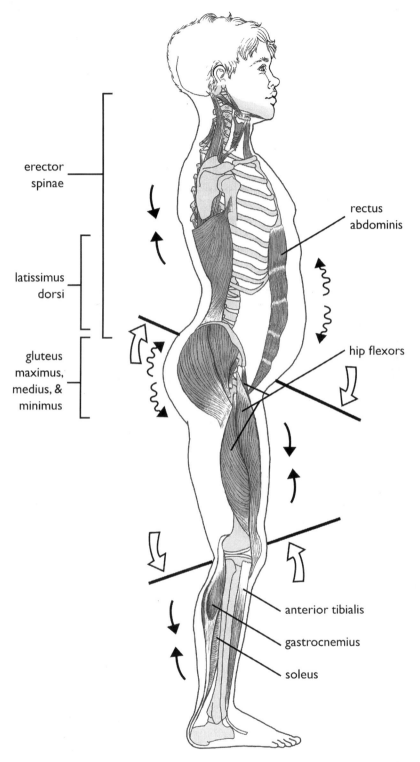

erector
spinae

latissimus
dorsi

gluteus
maximus,
medius, &
minimus

rectus
abdominis

hip flexors

anterior tibialis

gastrocnemius

soleus

Figure 1.9 In lower crossed syndrome, tightness in the lower back and weakness in the abdominal muscles yields diminished range of motion for the diaphragm and rib cage. *Sandy Escobar.*

Pronation Distortion Syndrome

Figure 1.10 shows how the hips, knees, and ankles are supported by optimal length/tension relationships between the leg muscles. Figure 1.11 shows how the muscular imbalances characteristic of pronation distortion syndrome impact these joints. Tightness in the hip adductors and calves and weakness in the gluteal and tibialis muscles result in an anterior pelvic tilt, internal rotation of the knees, and a turnout of the feet. The legs provide a base of support for the spine, so these impaired joint mechanics undermine postural stability in both stillness and motion. Well-balanced leg musculature is essential for securing breath management and maintaining vocal stability during stage movement, particularly when contending with a raked stage, heeled shoes, and/or challenging choreography.

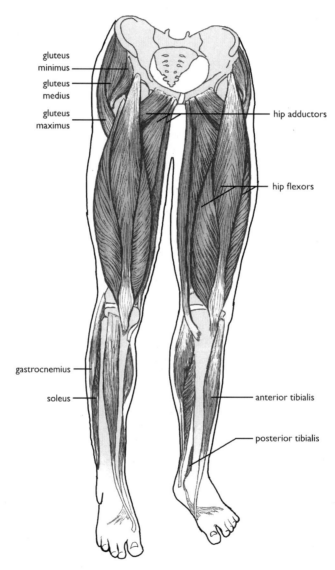

Figure 1.10 Good length/tension relationships between the leg muscles support joint function and overall stability. *Sandy Escobar.*

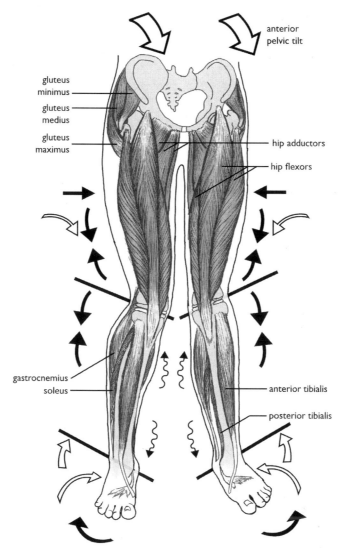

Figure 1.11 In pronation distortion syndrome, problematic length/tension relationships between the muscles that govern lower-body joint function can impact both breathing and movement. *Sandy Escobar.*

With the possible exception of some hard-core child athletes, everyone develops postural distortions and muscular imbalances. No one develops a perfectly balanced musculature by accident. Your body is the sum total of your habits and experiences. Distortions and imbalances can develop from holding static positions for significant periods of time. For example, maintaining the seated position necessary to drive a car long distances or work at a computer for hours can lead to the glutes becoming weak and the hip flexors tight; the resulting problematic muscle length and tension relationships can affect your gait.

While minor distortions and imbalances may create no problem whatsoever for the average human, serious athletes must strive to resolve them in order to achieve peak performance. A baseball player whose shoulder rotates internally will not be able to throw the ball as far or as fast as he or she would under more optimal conditions. A swimmer with weak gluteal muscles will not be able to kick with full range of motion through their hips. A singer who fails to address such muscular imbalances is essentially playing a dysfunctional instrument. The dysfunction may manifest visibly as only a subtly exaggerated spinal curvature or asymmetry, but it will almost certainly impact his or her singing in one or more ways.

Janda's three distortion patterns are useful examples of how common patterns of use can throw alignment out of balance. Resolving these distortions is key for fulfilling athletic potential of any kind. As each body is the result of a unique history, we are more likely to develop aspects of one or more rather than exactly conforming to any one pattern.

Assessing Your Alignment

The musculoskeletal system functions like a highly sophisticated, animated suspension bridge; our skeletal structure is like the towers that serve as the bridge's supports, while the muscles are like the cables that absorb the tensions of forces exerted on the bridge by gravity, vehicles, and wind. Muscles serve as levers that initiate joint action by contracting and moving the bones to which they are attached. We are able to accomplish this most efficiently when we enjoy optimal length/tension relationships between our muscles. Postural distortions are the consequence of imbalances in these muscular length/tension relationships—in other words, if one muscle that acts on a joint is tight while another is weak, the resulting imbalance will contribute to the kinds of postural distortions detailed in Janda's syndromes.

Here are two simple assessments that will help you check your alignment for muscular length/tension imbalances. The first assessment is static and the second dynamic. You can either have a friend photograph and film you or film yourself. Be sure to frame your whole body in each shot.

Static Alignment Assessment

Photograph yourself from the front and from the side. Stand with your feet about hip width apart, arms resting by your sides. Avoid the temptation to strike a pose based on any preconceptions you may have about good alignment—doing so will interfere with the accuracy of your assessment.

Figures 1.12 and 1.14 exemplify healthy alignment, while figures 1.13 and 1.15 demonstrate a variety of ways that postural imbalances can manifest. The horizontal and vertical lines shown in figures 1.12 and 1.14 indicate the checkpoints I recommend that you apply when observing and assessing your alignment.

FROM THE FRONT

- Is your head position neutral, or does it tilt toward one side or the other?

- Are your shoulders level with one another, or does one sit in a higher position than the other?

- Are your hips level with one another, or does one sit in a higher position than the other?

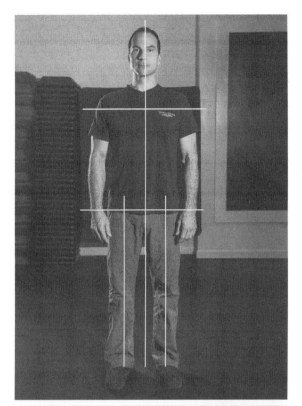

Figure 1.12 Balanced alignment viewed from the front. The head is centered; shoulders and hips are level; hips, knees and ankles align with each other; feet are parallel. *Daniel Welch.*

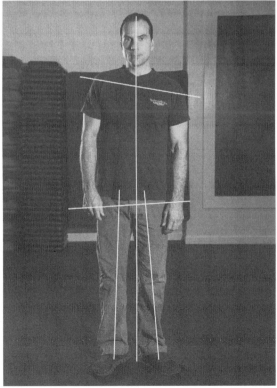

Figure 1.13 Distorted alignment. The head inclines towards the right shoulder, which is elevated relative to the left; the left hip is slightly elevated relative to the right; there is imperfect hip, knee and ankle alignment; the feet turn out. *Daniel Welch.*

Figure 1.14 Balanced alignment viewed from the side. The ear, shoulder, hip and ankle line up with one another. *Daniel Welch.*

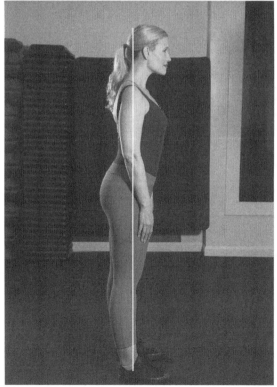

Figure 1.15 Distorted alignment. The ear is forward of the shoulder while the hip is well behind. *Daniel Welch.*

- Are your knees aligned with your hips and ankles, or do they rotate in toward each other or bow out to the sides?

- Are your feet parallel with toes pointing straight forward, or do they turn out to the side?

FROM THE SIDE

- Do your ears, shoulders, hips, and ankles align vertically?

- Is your head position neutral, or does your chin jut forward?

- Do your shoulders round forward?

- Is your lower back excessively arched, with your pelvis tilting forward?

- Are your knees neutral, or do they lock back?

Record your observations and evaluate your results:

- If your head tilts to one side, or if one of your shoulders is elevated relative to the other, this indicates an imbalance between the muscles on either side of your neck and shoulders.

- If your chin juts forward, this indicates tightness in your upper trapezius and levator scapulae and weakness in your neck flexors.

- If your shoulders rotate forward, this indicates tightness in your pectoral muscles and latissimus dorsi and weakness in your rhomboids and middle and lower trapezius.

- If one hip is elevated relative to the other, this indicates a muscular imbalance between the muscles of the lumbo-pelvic-hip complex on the left and right side.

- If your lower back is arched and your pelvis tilts forward, this indicates tightness in your latissimus dorsi, erector spinae, hip flexors, hip adductors, and calves, and weakness in your gluteus maximus, gluteus minimus, transversus abdominis, and internal obliques.

- If your knees rotate in toward one another and your feet turn out, this indicates tightness in your hamstrings, hip flexors, hip adductors, and calves, and weakness in your gluteus maximus, gluteus medius, hip external rotators, anterior tibialis, and posterior tibialis.

Dynamic Alignment Assessment

The movement for this assessment is called an overhead squat. Stand with your feet about hip width apart and your ankles, knees, and hips aligned. Raise your arms up in alignment with your ears, your elbows extended and palms facing one another, as shown in figures 1.16 and 1.18. Maintaining the raised arm position and a neutral spine, slowly squat as though you were about to sit down, as shown in figures 1.17 and 1.19. Only go as low as you can comfortably keep your balance, then smoothly reverse the movement and return to your starting position. Repeat this movement several times while filming yourself from both the front and the side. View your movements and record your observations.

Figure 1.16 Overhead squat, starting position. *Sandy Escobar.*

Figure 1.17 Overhead squat, movement. *Sandy Escobar.*

Complete Vocal Fitness

Figure 1.18 Overhead squat, starting position. *Sandy Escobar.*

Figure 1.19 Overhead squat, movement. *Sandy Escobar.*

FROM THE FRONT

- Do your knees remain aligned with your hips and ankles throughout the movement, or do they move in toward the center or out toward the sides?

- Are your feet parallel, or do they turn out?

- Does your weight appear to be evenly distributed between your feet throughout the movement, or do you shift your weight to one side?

FROM THE SIDE

- Does your spine remain neutral on the descent, or does your lower back arch or round?

- Does your spine move parallel to your lower leg on the descent, or does your torso excessively lean forward?

- Do your arms remain aligned with your ears, or do they fall forward?

Evaluate your results:

- If your body shifts to one side on the descent, this indicates an imbalance between the muscles of your core and legs on either side, as shown in figure 1.20.

- If your knees move in toward the center on the descent, this indicates tightness in your hip adductors and calves and weakness in your gluteus maximus, gluteus medius, anterior tibialis, and posterior tibialis, as shown in figure 1.21.

- If your knees move out toward the sides on the descent, this indicates tightness in your hamstrings and gluteus minimus and weakness in your gluteus maximus and hip adductors.

- If your feet turn out on the descent, this indicates tightness in your calves and hamstrings and weakness in your gluteus maximus and gluteus medius, as shown in figure 1.21.

- If your lower back arches on the descent, this indicates tightness in your latissimus dorsi, erector spinae, and hip flexors, and weakness in your gluteus maximus, hamstrings, and core, as shown in figure 1.22.

- If your lower back rounds on the descent, this indicates tightness in your hamstrings, rectus abdominis, and external obliques, and weakness in your gluteus maximus, erector spinae, latissimus dorsi, hip flexors, and core.

- If your torso leans forward excessively on the descent, this indicates tightness in your abdominal muscles, hip flexors, and calves and weakness in your erector spinae, gluteus maximus, transversus abdominis, and anterior tibialis, as shown in figure 1.23.

- If your arms fall forward, this indicates tightness in your pectoral muscles and latissimus dorsi and weakness in your rhomboids, middle and lower trapezius, and posterior deltoid.

Figure 1.20 Overhead squat: weight shifts to one side on the descent. *Sandy Escobar.*

Figure 1.21 Overhead squat: knees rotate internally and feet turn out. *Sandy Escobar.*

Figure 1.22 Overhead squat: lower back arches. *Sandy Escobar.*

Figure 1.23 Overhead squat: excessive forward lean. *Sandy Escobar.*

Corrective Exercise Protocols

The term "corrective exercise" refers to fitness program design strategies aimed at assessing and resolving imbalances in order to improve overall function, as opposed to programs emphasizing muscle gain or weight loss as ends in themselves. The assessments and strategies offered in this chapter have been adapted from the corrective exercise protocols developed by the National Academy of Sports Medicine. NASM advocates a four-step procedure for addressing muscular imbalances:

1. Release muscles that are relatively tight.

2. Stretch muscles that are relatively tight.

3. Strengthen, in isolation, muscles that are relatively weak in order to activate them.

4. Integrate the movements of these newly activated muscles by training them in the context of whole-body movements.

Release and Lengthen Tight Muscles

If you want to improve your alignment, you must improve mobility in the various structures that hold you in your default position. This is most effectively accomplished by releasing tight muscles prior to performing static stretches. The muscular release technique I advocate throughout this book is called self-myofascial release, a method employing a foam roller, ball, or massage stick to loosen and restructure the web of connective tissue that surrounds muscles and connects them to one another and to the skeletal system. Static stretching has been shown to be more effective after a muscle group has first been released by applying this technique.

Strengthen and Integrate Weak Muscles

Muscles can develop weakness from being underutilized and/or as a result of synergistic dominance. Synergistic dominance is the result of learning to perform movements not with the muscles best positioned for the job but rather with their "synergists"— smaller muscles that are positioned to help with the movement in question that readily compensate when the primary mover fails to do the lion's share of the work. For example, if you want to push something heavy, the large pectoral muscles in your chest are the ones best equipped for the assignment. But, if they are underdeveloped, then your triceps—their synergists—will take over. In such a case, it is important to perform isolated strengthening movements to activate your pectoral muscles, because if you attempt a more complex movement such as a push-up, your triceps may do the work instead. Once your pecs have been activated, it becomes important to engage them within the context of more complex movements, perhaps involving your core and legs as well as your triceps.

Emphasize Balance and Stabilization

One of Janda's major innovations in postural rehabilitation was the introduction of stabilization training to restore muscular balance and functional movement. One of the principles of an effective corrective exercise protocol is the directive to perform movements in as unstable an environment as one is ready to handle. This includes such things as engaging limbs independently from one another, rather than both arms or legs simultaneously; prioritizing exercises employing body weight and free-moving tools like dumbbells and cables, rather than stable weight-lifting machines; and performing movements on an unstable surface or while standing on one leg. These strategies are key for evening out strength imbalances not only around each joint but also between your right and left sides.

Stabilization training is of particularly high sport-specific value for singers. The ability to stabilize the shoulders and core is essential for breath management, as I will discuss in chapter 2. The ability to stabilize the lumbo-pelvic-hip complex confers an ability to engage in stage movement without allowing leg movement to interfere with breath management or crucial activities in and around your throat.

———————

Alignment plays as significant a role in singing as it does for every other athletic endeavor. If, despite diligent and sustained technical work, you find that you are still unable to access your full range, manage your breath adequately, or achieve balanced resonance, it may be due to postural rather than technical imbalances. Fortunately, these imbalances can be systematically resolved. You will find that doing so not only supports your singing but also improves overall wellness and mitigates the challenges that can attend the frequent air travel, unfamiliar sleeping conditions, and interesting staging choices that often end up being part of your job.

2

Breathing

Life begins at the moment of our first breath and extends to the moment we breathe our last. Breathing unites us with the world around us in perpetual symbiosis as we inhale oxygen and exhale carbon dioxide. Breathing massages our internal organs, promoting healthy digestion and supporting the lymphatic system. Breathing regulates our emotions, heightening excitement or calming us down as needed. Human beings can survive three weeks without food, three days without water, but little more than three minutes without breathing.

While each component of the singer's instrument has numerous physical functions to fulfill in addition to singing, our breathing apparatus is responsible for an exceptional range of jobs relating to survival, comfort, and expression. The many ways in which breathing contributes to keeping us alive and well hardly diminish in significance once we begin to vocalize. The physical roles breath plays in supporting our bodily functions and regulating the flow of our emotions are as vital for the realization of our expressive impulses as the mechanical role breath plays as the generator of sound for the vocal instrument.

Breath as Generator

All musical instruments require a means of generating sound. A violin's strings are set vibrating by the movement of a bow, a piano's strings respond to hammer strikes initiated by fingers, and a singer's vocal folds are activated by the breath. For any instrument, an effective generator provides for consistency, stamina, and variable intensity of sound production. Singers must therefore cultivate the ability to control and vary airflow and subglottal breath pressure with great specificity. As our breath is limited by our lung capacity, it is a resource that must be deployed economically and then skillfully renewed upon depletion.

Breathing for singing can be broken down into four distinct but related skills, each of which must be mastered for the breath to serve as an effective generator:

- The ability to take a full breath

- The ability to release the breath freely

- The ability to optimize and manage subglottal breath pressure

- The ability to consume oxygen efficiently.

Ability to Take a Full Breath

When we inhale, we contract the muscles of inspiration. These include the diaphragm and intercostal muscles. Figures 2.1 and 2.3 show the relationship of the ribs, diaphragm, and intercostal muscles prior to inhalation; figures 2.2 and 2.4 show how their positions evolve in response to a deep inhalation.

The diaphragm is the primary muscle of inspiration. This dome-shaped structure nestles under the lungs. The diaphragm attaches to the xyphoid process of the sternum as well as the lower ribs and spine, separating the thoracic cavity from the abdominal cavity. The two crura of the diaphragm, shown in figures 2.1 to 2.4, originate in the lumbar vertebrae and serve as anchors for muscular contraction. When activated, the diaphragm descends as shown in figures 2.2 and 2.4, drawing air into the lungs by creating a vacuum in the thoracic cavity and displacing the viscera.

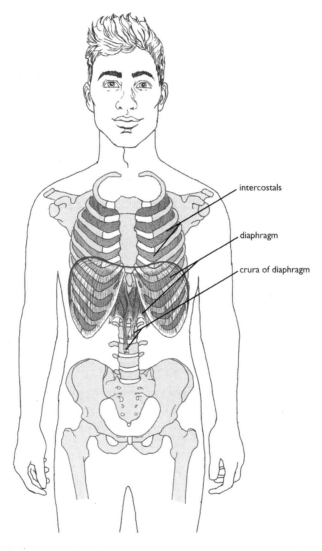

Figure 2.1 Front view of the ribs, diaphragm, and intercostals prior to inhalation. *Sandy Escobar.*

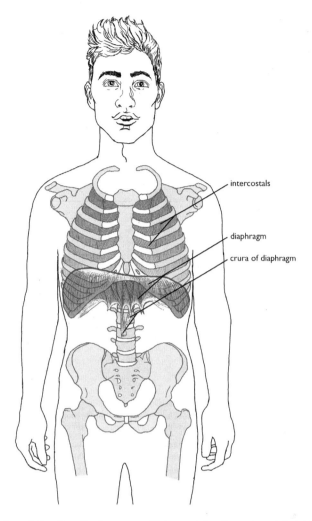

intercostals

diaphragm

crura of diaphragm

Figure 2.2 Front view of the ribs, diaphragm, and intercostals after a deep inhalation. *Sandy Escobar.*

The intercostals are the muscles between the ribs. On inspiration, they lift and separate the ribs, which hinge on the sternum in front and the spine in the back, as shown in figures 2.2 and 2.4, partnering with the diaphragm to create a vacuum and draw air into the lungs.

Both our control over the diaphragm and our ability to sense its movements are indirect. While the intention to inhale activates the diaphragm, we cannot exercise direct biomechanical control over its movements. We are only able to sense its whereabouts from the feedback we receive from its neighboring structures and an awareness of pressure changes in the thoracic and abdominal cavities.

Inspiration can be both voluntary and involuntary. When we wish to consciously modulate our breath, as in singing and many forms of physical exercise, we can deliberately inhale and exhale, as well as vary the speed and depth of both movements. At all other times, breathing automatically continues unconsciously, regulated by the nervous system. For singers, the ability to take a full breath means:

- Accessing the fullest possible range of motion for the diaphragm and intercostals.

- An absence of resistance in the throat and other airways.

- The ability to allow the shoulders to remain relaxed and settled while inhaling.

Factors that can impede the ability to take a full breath include:

- Postural distortions limiting range of motion for the diaphragm and intercostals, as discussed in chapter 1.

- Resistance in the throat that manifests as an audible inhalation.

- Habitual or chronic tensions in the chest and/or abdomen.

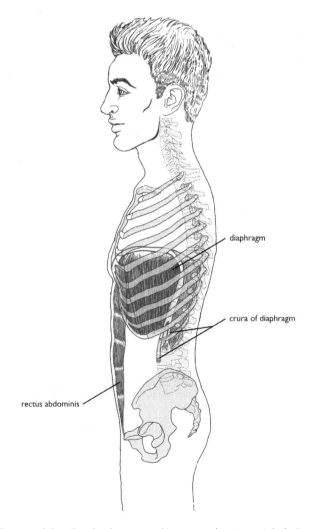

Figure 2.3 Side view of the ribs, diaphragm, and intercostals prior to inhalation. *Sandy Escobar.*

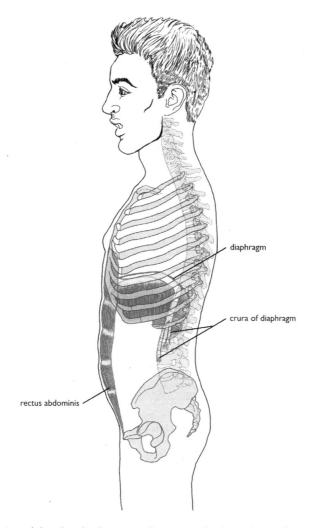

diaphragm

crura of diaphragm

rectus abdominis

Figure 2.4 Side view of the ribs, diaphragm, and intercostals after a deep inhalation. *Sandy Escobar.*

While not every phrase you sing may require filling your lungs to capacity, it is vital that you enjoy the freedom and flexibility to maximally inhale so that you have the option to breathe as fully or minimally as desired. Optimizing alignment supports full range of motion for the diaphragm and intercostals and can be cultivated by adapting the workout regimen detailed in chapter 6 for your specific postural needs. The static stretches for the rib cage are particularly helpful for releasing tensions in the intercostals and abdominal muscles.

Throat tensions that result in an audible gasp impede the flow of inhalation and can be alleviated through slow, mindful, repeated practice. In my experience, singers are far more inclined to practice the movements that produce sound than they are to practice the movements involved in inhalation, but the things you do to prepare to sing are every bit as important as the things you do while singing. You can habituate silent inhalations through a relaxed throat by slowing down the process, inhaling out of tempo, then gradually building the coordination to accomplish this movement more swiftly. The "turn your breath around" exercise described below addresses this procedure in greater detail.

Breathing

While the shoulders normally elevate during inhalation and settle during exhalation, singers must cultivate the ability to allow the shoulders to remain low during inhalation rather than elevating them. Elevating the shoulders engages the upper trapezius. This tightens the neck and shoulder muscles in the back and on both sides and draws the shoulders up and in toward the neck, potentially causing problems for laryngeal mobility and stability. The scapular retraction exercise described below helps stabilize the shoulders and improve awareness of and control over the upper trapezius.

Habitual tensions, such as the common tendency to suck in your stomach, must be observed and consciously released. Some degree of engagement of the abdominal muscles is necessary to support alignment and movement, and some further engagement may be cultivated as a component of your singing technique. But unconscious holding in this area will restrict the diaphragm's ability to displace the viscera on inhalation and limit your ability to fully expand your lungs. The static stretches for the rib cage described in chapter 6 also help lengthen and release the abdominal muscles.

Chronic muscular tensions in the torso, such as the tightness in the pectoral and latissimus dorsi muscles that is characteristic of upper crossed syndrome, can be alleviated through the self-myofascial release and flexibility exercises detailed in chapter 6.

Ability to Release the Breath Freely

When we exhale, we passively release the muscles of inspiration.

The diaphragm contracts when we inhale and releases when we exhale, returning to a relaxed position as shown in figures 2.1 and 2.2. During normal exhalation, the same is true of its synergists, the intercostals. While the intercostals, as well as many other muscles throughout the torso, can be engaged to forcefully expel the air in our lungs, the skill under discussion in this section is simply that of allowing the air to passively release.

The tissue that makes up our lungs is similar in quality to the rubber used in balloons. Inhaling expands and stretches this tissue, which is then naturally inclined to return to a relaxed state. The passive expiratory force generated by the natural elasticity of our lung tissue is more formidable than any active muscular action we can take to expel our air—something to keep in mind when developing breath-management strategies, as discussed below.

When you consider that the diaphragm relaxes rather than contracts on exhalation, it becomes clear that admonitions to "sing from your diaphragm" or "engage your diaphragm" are anatomically incorrect and misleading. The diaphragm has one job, and that is to contract on inhalation, whereas singing is an activity of exhalation. If it feels like you are "singing from the diaphragm," you are likely feeling the abdominal muscles. These intersect with the diaphragm in the front at the sternum and lower ribs (see figure 2.8, below) but given that you cannot directly control or sense the diaphragm and that it is relaxed during exhalation, it is more probable that you are engaging and sensing your abdominal muscles. For singers, the ability to release the breath freely means:

- After a full inhalation, the ability to let the breath go without creating resistance in the throat, controlling the rate of release, or actively doing anything to push the breath out

- The ability to maintain good alignment of the shoulders and sternum rather than allowing them to collapse

- The ability to seamlessly turn the breath around after completing the exhalation, rather than pausing and holding the breath prior to the next inhalation

Factors that can impede the ability to release the breath include:

- Habitual or chronic tensions in the rib cage or throat impeding a full, swift exhalation

- Allowing the sternum and/or shoulders to collapse due to weakness in the rhomboids and middle/lower trapezius

- A tendency to either push the breath out or modulate its release rather than passively letting it go

- A habit of pausing and holding the breath on completion of the exhalation

While your approach to singing technique may involve exercising control over the rate at which your breath releases, the ability to simply let it go in a complete and uncomplicated fashion is a prerequisite for the development of breath-management skills. Any pushing or controlling you may be doing unintentionally or unconsciously will slow or limit your progress in breath management, so it's important to note and resolve such tendencies early.

During normal exhalation, the shoulders generally descend and rotate internally and the sternum also descends, but singers must cultivate the ability to stabilize the shoulders while releasing the breath; many singing techniques call for sustaining an elevated position of the sternum as well. Figure 2.5 shows the scapulae at rest. Maintaining shoulder stability, which also contributes to sustaining an elevated sternum, requires retraction of the scapulae, shown in figure 2.6; however, a tendency to elevate the shoulders on inspiration, as shown in figure 2.7, makes it impossible to either stabilize the shoulders or keep the sternum up. Good default alignment is necessary for accomplishing this, as well as strength in the muscles that stabilize the scapulae—the rhomboids and middle and lower trapezius, shown in figure 2.9 (later in the chapter). The scapular retraction exercise described below helps stabilize the shoulders and maintain an elevated sternum while exhaling.

A habit of pausing and holding the breath on completion of the exhalation puts the whole breathing cycle on hold, taking up valuable time between phrases and requiring additional effort to initiate the inhalation that follows. Such pauses can be accompanied by a habitual tightening in the throat and/or abdominal muscles. Practice exhaling, then seamlessly transitioning to inhaling without a pause. The "turn your breath around" exercise described below applies this process to the performance of consecutive phrases.

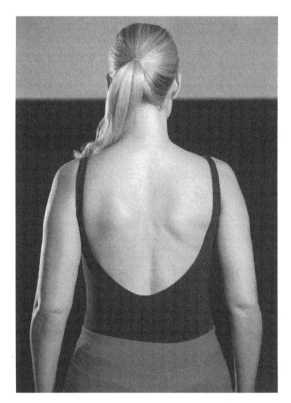

Figure 2.5 Relaxed shoulders. *Daniel Welch.*

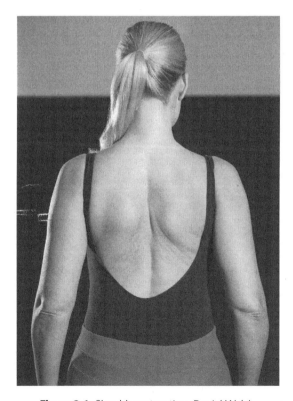

Figure 2.6 Shoulder retraction. *Daniel Welch.*

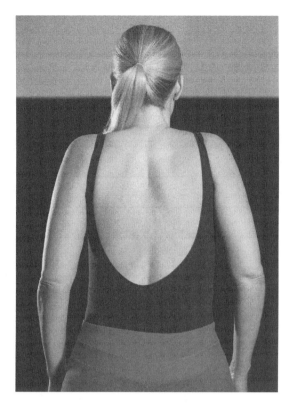

Figure 2.7 Shoulder elevation. *Daniel Welch.*

Ability to Optimize Subglottal Breath Pressure

The breath generates vocal fold vibration in accordance with the Bernoulli principle. After a full inhalation, the air pressure below the vocal folds is greater than the air pressure above them, so when the vocal folds are sufficiently adducted while remaining pliant, releasing breath through the resulting narrow aperture alternately sucks them together and escapes between them, generating a vibratory cycle.

The process of inhalation creates adequate subglottal breath pressure to generate this vibratory cycle during exhalation due to the elasticity of our lung tissue. Breath management for singing therefore consists of a means of increasing and regulating subglottal breath pressure to facilitate a greater and/or more specific impact on vocal fold vibration in order to modulate volume, projection, and registration.

Enhancing subglottal breath pressure means exercising control over the degree of concentration, or compression, of the air molecules inside your lungs. We have a variety of means to accomplish this. Most muscles in the torso are capable of playing primarily an inspiratory or expiratory role, either by directly influencing the rib cage or by impacting intra-abdominal pressure, which also influences pressure inside the thoracic cavity. Muscles that play an expiratory role will accelerate the rate at which breath exits our lungs, while muscles that play an inspiratory role will decelerate the rate of release. If we wish to influence the air compression inside our lungs, we must harness and skillfully balance these forces of acceleration and deceleration.

Forces that accelerate breath release include anything that can act on the lungs to push the air out, including the abdominal muscles (shown in figure 2.8), the intercostal muscles, and any muscles or movements that cause the sternum to descend (figure 2.9).

Forces that decelerate breath release include anything that can hold the air back, including continued engagement of the muscles of inspiration, such as the diaphragm and the intercostal muscles. Engaging the rhomboids and lower and middle trapezius, shown in figure 2.8, to stabilize the shoulders and elevate the sternum assists with continued engagement of the intercostals. Anything that slows the release of the breath by creating resistance in or around the glottis will also exercise a decelerating force. This includes the normal approximation of the vocal folds during phonation. Exaggerated adduction of the vocal folds will further decelerate the rate of breath release, as will the creation of additional throat tension around the larynx.

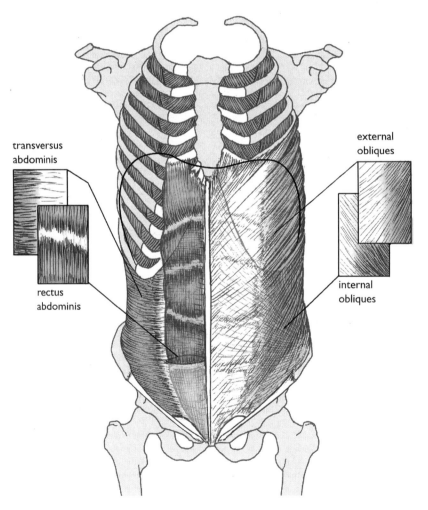

Figure 2.8 The four major abdominal muscles: transversus abdominis, rectus abdominis, external obliques, and internal obliques. All have significant attachments to the rib cage and influence breathing in myriad ways. *Sandy Escobar.*

Pairing and coordinating forces that accelerate and decelerate the rate of breath release facilitate the concentration and compression of the breath, impacting subglottal breath pressure. As you can see, there are many muscles that can exercise each of these forces, and I believe that this is the reason for the evolution of so many different schools of breath management. For example, bel canto aficionados recommend sustained expansion of the rib cage (deceleration) combined with an upward tuck of the abdominal muscles (acceleration); adherents of the German school of breathing advise continuously distending the abdomen (deceleration) while singing, requiring the sternum and ribs to draw in and down (acceleration).

Given the variety of options we have for regulating subglottal breath pressure, I find it unlikely that any one method could be demonstrated to be superior to any other. However, there is one principle that must hold true for any successful means of breath management: Never recruit anatomy whose primary role in the vocal instrument is something other than generator to play the role of the generator. In other words, you must not engage the structures in and around the larynx (vibrator) or articulators (resonator) for the purpose of increasing subglottal breath pressure.

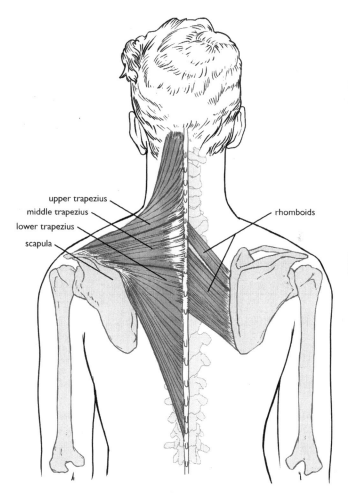

Figure 2.9 Upper trapezius, rhomboids, and middle and lower trapezius. The upper trapezius elevates the shoulders; the rhomboids and middle and lower trapezius retract and stabilize the scapulae. *Sandy Escobar.*

I feel that this cannot be overstated, because the most instinctive and expedient way to increase subglottal breath pressure is by generating tension in the throat, usually by excessively adducting the vocal folds (deceleration) and driving the breath against this closure with the abdominal and/or intercostal muscles (acceleration). Doing so will effectively increase subglottal breath pressure, but at the expense of laryngeal function, as your laryngeal anatomy and the structures surrounding it will no longer be adequately available to perform their roles in vibration and resonance. Your vocal folds will not be able to vibrate or modulate pitch and registration as freely if they are also responsible for creating resistance for the breath to push against. Subjecting your vocal folds to prolonged and excessive breath pressure can also increase the risk of vocal fold hemorrhage or the development of nodes or polyps.

This is my reason for preferring the term *breath management* to *support*. I find that singers too often respond to the word *support* by engaging the forces that accelerate the breath while possibly failing to notice that they are using these forces to override excessive resistance at the glottis—some of which may be due to an underdeveloped technique rather than an intentional means of breath management.

Chapter 6 will include exercises to improve flexibility, strength, and coordination throughout the musculature that impacts breathing, in order to facilitate the application of whatever breath-management strategy works best for you. The scapular retraction exercise described below helps strengthen a number of the muscles capable of decelerating breath release by enabling the shoulders, sternum, and thoracic spine to sustain an inspiratory position.

Ability to Consume Oxygen Efficiently

The primary function of respiration is the delivery of oxygen to our cells and elimination of carbon dioxide from our bodies. Our level of cardiorespiratory fitness is defined by how well our bodies accomplish these tasks. The efficiency with which we are able to circulate oxygen through our bodies and then make good use of that oxygen contributes our overall level of energy and physical stamina.

Our bodies do not consume all of the oxygen we take in with each breath. This is why it is possible to deliver oxygen to another person when administering rescue breaths during cardiopulmonary resuscitation (CPR)—there is still a significant quantity of oxygen in the air we exhale.

The positive adaptations our bodies undergo as the result of cardiorespiratory training include an increase in stroke volume—the quantity of blood our hearts pump with each beat—and an improvement in oxygen consumption due to an increase in capillary and mitochondrial density. When your heart becomes capable of pumping more blood every time it beats, it circulates not only a greater volume of blood but also a greater quantity of oxygen through your body with each beat. A greater stroke volume results in a lower resting heart rate because your heart no longer needs to beat as frequently. As a consequence, you do not need to breathe as frequently. An increase in capillary density provides more pathways for oxygen to reach your tissues; an increase in mitochondrial density provides more locations for oxygen to interact with the nutrients you consume in order to supply your body with energy.

Simply put, the more efficiently you consume oxygen, the less frequently you need to breathe.

An improvement in oxygen consumption raises your overall level of energy and stamina. In addition, it yields two highly desirable advantages for your singing:

1. The ability to sustain long phrases, and

2. The ability to continue singing calmly and skillfully throughout vigorous stage movement.

If you've ever felt like you were running out of breath despite seeming to have plenty of air in your lungs, it is likely due to your having depleted all the oxygen you were capable of consuming from your last breath. This generates an emergency signal from your body to inhale as soon as possible. Better oxygen consumption translates into greater latitude for your musicanship because it enables you to sustain longer phrases as well as regulate dynamics and modulate registration with greater skill. Everything for which you rely on breath management becomes easier.

Your respiratory system's main job is delivering oxygen so it can be converted into the energy you need to function. Movement places further demands upon your respiratory system, and singing still more. An increase in physical activity means an increase in energy expenditure, necessitating more frequent breaths as well as more frequent heartbeats. The frequency of a singer's breaths is necessarily dictated by the number and length of the phrases that must be performed over a given period of time. Therefore, it is essential that you cultivate a level of oxygen consumption adequate to meet the demands of stage movement without necessitating more frequent breaths than would be ideal for your musical and dramatic delivery. Interval training, an excellent means of improving oxygen consumption, will be discussed in chapter 6.

Exercises for Breath Coordination

In the introduction to this book, I described sport-specific training as comprising strength and flexibility exercises, to be carried out in the gym, and coordination and skill exercises, which are cultivated in the field (aka the practice room where our sport is concerned). You will find exercises to condition your breathing musculature in chapter 6. Following are two breathing coordination exercises that you can incorporate into your vocal practice regimen.

Exercise: Scapular Retraction

The rhomboids and middle and lower trapezius stabilize the shoulders by retracting the scapulae. Sustaining this retracted position is beneficial for singing because it helps maintain an elevated sternum while inhibiting the upper trapezius from elevating the shoulders. Here is a procedure for improving awareness and coordination in this crucial area.

1. Warm up your shoulders with the following exercises from chapter 6:

   • Self-myofascial release for the shoulders

   • Massage for the upper trapezius

   • Half-angel stretch for the shoulders

2. Explore the impact of your shoulder muscles on your alignment:

   - Stand with good alignment.

   - Slouch by allowing your chest to collapse and your shoulders to slump forward.

   - Slowly draw yourself back into a position of good alignment.

   - Repeat several times, noting where you sensed the effort. The muscles that restore you to good alignment include the muscles between your shoulder blades—the rhomboids and middle/lower trapezius. When these muscles are weak or lengthened, the result is a slouch.

3. Practice scapular retraction:

   - Sit upright on a padded workout bench, massage table, or other firm upholstered surface.

   - Make fists with your hands and place them beside your hips, knuckles against the surface you are seated upon.

   - Maintaining good upper-body alignment with your sternum elevated, raise your hips off the surface by pushing yourself up onto your fists. This will cause your scapulae to retract.

   - Keep your weight on your fists for two to four seconds, continuing to breathe; then lower yourself and return to a seated position.

   - Repeat four to six times.

4. Integrate scapular retraction into the lat pulldown exercise in chapter 6.

The purpose of these exercises is to permanently strengthen the rhomboids and middle/lower trapezius to promote good alignment, as well as to habituate dynamic shoulder stabilization during singing. Remember to keep your shoulders loose and available for movement—the point of these exercises is never the promotion of a rigid or held position but rather a balance of strength and flexibility throughout the skeletomuscular system.

Exercise: Turning the Breath Around

Singers who tirelessly work their best technique, diction, and musicianship into the performance of each individual phrase often do not invest similar time and attention to choreographing their breaths—the way they release a phrase, inhale, prepare, and initiate the subsequent phrase. No matter how efficient and well-coordinated your breath-management skills, they will only serve you well in performance if you intentionally apply these skills to the transitions between phrases in your repertoire. You must also ensure that the instinctive urge to come in "on time" does not override your preparation.

While composers do not always notate rests of sufficient length for breathing between phrases, they still expect you to take the time you need in order to breathe and prepare well. The composer, your pianist or conductor, and everyone listening *knows* that breathing takes time. It is up to you to build the breath you need into the overall flow of musical expression so that it feels organic.

I frequently observe singers taking a noisy catch breath an eighth or quarter note before an entrance even when they are provided rests a full measure or more in length to prepare, essentially treating the breath as a rhythmic event. However, under nearly all circumstances while singing, *breathing should be regarded as completely arhythmic*. If you have a break of a measure or more before an entrance, you must choose the moment where you will begin to prepare for that entrance based on how long it will take you to inhale adequately rather than on rhythmic concerns. When you do not have a lengthy break, remember that while performing you should always be either singing or inhaling (never holding your breath), so your inhalation and preparation must occupy whatever rhythmic duration you are allotted in the space between phrases. If there are no rests between phrases, or only short ones, you must exercise good judgment and shorten the last note of the previous phrase so that you have the time you need to prepare well and come in on time when the subsequent one is set to begin. Here is an exercise sequence for turning your breath around between phrases.

Breathing without vocalizing. Stand with good alignment and a relaxed jaw. Relax your throat, shoulders, and abdomen and take a full breath through your mouth. Exhale through your mouth, taking care to release rather than push your breath out. When you have finished exhaling, seamlessly turn your breath around and begin to inhale, again encouraging your throat, shoulders, and abdomen to relax; then seamlessly turn your breath around and exhale. Repeat the cycle several times. Observe:

- Do your throat, shoulders, and abdomen remain relaxed, or do you find it necessary to release some accumulated tension in these or other areas when you resume inhaling?

- Are you able to seamlessly transition between inhaling and exhaling, or are you inclined to pause and hold your breath briefly in between?

Onsets and releases. Stand with good alignment and a relaxed jaw. Relax your throat, shoulders, and abdomen, and take a full breath through your mouth. When you are ready to exhale, turn your breath around seamlessly as you did in the previous exercise, and onset on a comfortable pitch in your middle voice on the vowel of your choice. Sustain for two to three seconds, release the pitch, and inhale again. Repeat the cycle several times. Observe:

- Do your throat, shoulders, and abdomen remain relaxed as you onset and sustain, or do you find it necessary to release tension in these or other areas in order to inhale?

- Are you able to seamlessly transition between inhaling and onseting, releasing and inhaling, or is there a pause or some tightening unrelated to singing in between?

- Note and try to inhibit or release any extraneous movements and tensions interfering with a seamless turnaround between your inhalation and your onset or between your release and subsequent inhalation.

Application to repertoire. Choose two consecutive phrases in a song or aria with either no notated rest or only a brief notated rest in between.

- Onset on the final pitch and vowel of the first phrase.

- Sustain for two to three seconds.

- Release and seamlessly transition to a full inhalation.

- Onset on the first pitch and vowel of the second phrase.

- Sustain for two or three seconds.

- Release and seamlessly transition to a full inhalation.

- Repeat the cycle several times, alternating between the two pitches and vowels required.

- Sing through both phrases, taking adequate time for an optimal breath.

- Sing through both phrases, taking the time in between them that would be appropriate for performance.

- Compare your breath coordination between the version where you allowed yourself ample time to breathe and prepare and the version where you allowed yourself only as much time as would be appropriate in performance. Did additional tensions creep in when a time constraint was imposed? Was your breath silent and full or comparatively audible and shallow?

Breathing takes time, but you can improve your coordination to ensure that it does not take any more time than is necessary. Like any other movement sequence, practicing the movements involved in breathing will enable you to accomplish them with increased speed and efficiency.

Just as our life experiences lead most of us to develop idiosyncratic postural imbalances, each of us evolves unique breathing patterns. If you address the habits that impede range of motion for your ribs and diaphragm while building flexibility and strength in the muscles governing breath management, you will more readily cultivate the breath coordination and management skills you practice in the studio. And the better your level of cardiorespiratory fitness, the more stamina you will enjoy not only for your singing but also for everything else you pursue.

3

Laryngeal Function

As a graduate student, I failed to grasp laryngeal anatomy in any practically applicable sense. I was able to learn basic terminology and concepts well enough to fulfill course requirements and pass exams but not well enough for them to inform the way I taught. It was only some years after I completed my doctorate and decided to pursue certification as a fitness trainer that I learned functional anatomy in a way that informed and advanced my pedagogy.

My work as a trainer required that I understand the basics of the human movement system in order to apply this information to teach people how to become stronger, more flexible, and better coordinated. Through observing ankles, hips, and shoulders in action, day in and day out, I became adept at recognizing dysfunctional movement patterns and designing programs to help my clients establish healthier biomechanics.

As I became more skillful at analyzing and working with the external movements of physical exercise, I began to more deeply comprehend the complex internal movements that occur in and around the larynx when we sing.

The education I received while preparing for fitness certification also helped me realize why vocal anatomy can be so difficult to grasp for even the most dedicated student. I imagine that music majors seldom study biology beyond a high school level, and even college-level biology textbooks do not cover human anatomy and movement. This means that our very first exposure to anatomical vocabulary and concepts such as flexion, extension, adduction, origin and attachment points of muscles, and so on, takes place in relation to extraordinarily complex structures like the larynx or diaphragm, viewed with little or no reference to the overall musculoskeletal system. Attempting to thus master such information is like trying to start a video game at the expert level, without even being offered a diagram of the controller. But at least when you're playing a video game there is a chance that figuring it all out will afford you some pleasure. By contrast, the anatomical information in your vocal pedagogy texts may have only minimal overlap with the language your teacher employs in the studio, and therefore no discernable application for your technique. And voice students cannot be expected to devote valuable time to anything that doesn't promise to help them sing better, especially something as esoteric as anatomy.

Symbols appearing in brackets are drawn from the International Phonetic Alphabet. IPA is the pronunciation guide in common use by classical singers that notates the sounds of language.

An understanding of laryngeal function can indeed help you learn to sing better, provided that you have the means to relate that understanding to your singing practice with the same directness with which a trainer applies knee kinematics to promote good squat form. In this chapter it is my aim to introduce the structures comprising laryngeal anatomy within the context of their roles in creating vibration, varying pitch, and modulating registration, as well as to offer strategies for optimizing their function.

Vocal Fold Vibration

The vocal folds are composed of mucous membrane and serve as the vibrator for the vocal instrument. They attach in the front to a single point located inside the thyroid cartilage just below the Adam's apple and at the back to the arytenoid cartilages. The posterior cricoarytenoid muscles abduct (pull apart) the arytenoid cartilages, causing the vocal folds to open as shown in figure 3.1. The lateral cricoarytenoid muscles adduct (draw together) the arytenoid cartilages, causing the vocal folds to approximate as shown in figure 3.2.

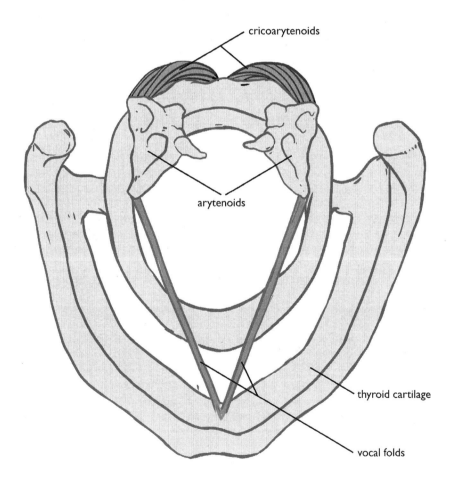

Figure 3.1 Vocal folds abducted. *Sandy Escobar.*

The aperture between the vocal folds is also called the glottis. The two primary roles of glottal closure in human anatomy are preventing foreign objects (such as food) from entering the trachea, and stabilizing the torso. When the glottis is tightly closed such that no air can escape, the resulting pressure stabilization within the thoracic and abdominal cavities facilitates lifting heavy objects; it also aids in defecation. While the glottis originally evolved to accomplish such activities, now that it has further evolved to become capable of nuanced musical vibration it is my recommendation that you employ other muscle groups to generate the internal stability needed for lifting and defecating.

As discussed in chapter 2, vocal fold vibration is stimulated by the release of the breath in accordance with the Bernoulli principle. When the aperture between the vocal folds is sufficiently narrow and the vocal folds themselves are sufficiently supple, the differential in the air pressure below and above causes them to alternately approximate and come apart in a regular vibratory pattern.

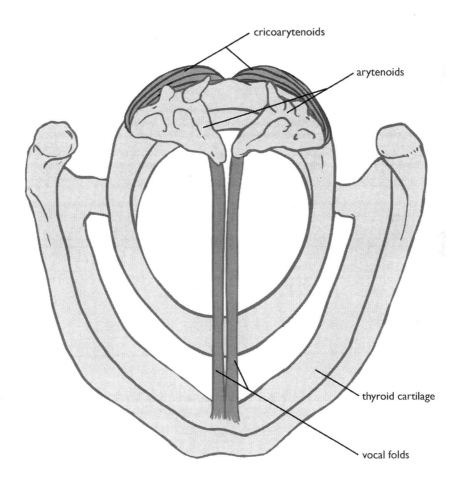

Figure 3.2 Vocal folds adducted. *Sandy Escobar.*

Pitch and Registration

The vocal folds are extraordinarily malleable structures, capable of varying length and thickness. Elongating the vocal folds results in the production of higher pitches; shortening them lowers the pitch. Thickening the vocal folds results in heavier registration, while thinning them lightens registration.

The muscles that modulate pitch and registration are the thyroarytenoid muscles (figures 3.3 and 3.4) and the cricothyroid muscles (figure 3.5).

The Thyroarytenoids

The thyroarytenoids are the muscular components of the vocal folds themselves. When they contract, as shown in figure 3.4, they shorten and thicken the vocal folds, lowering pitch and increasing the weight of registration.

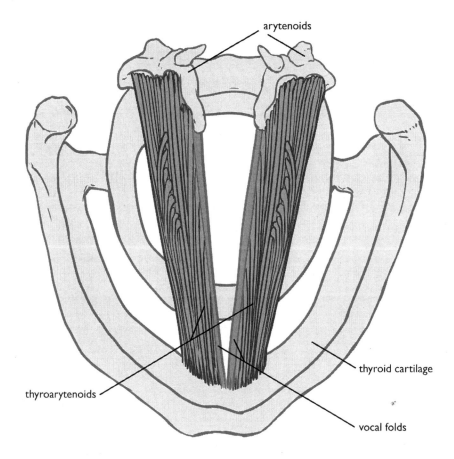

Figure 3.3 Thyroarytenoids. *Sandy Escobar.*

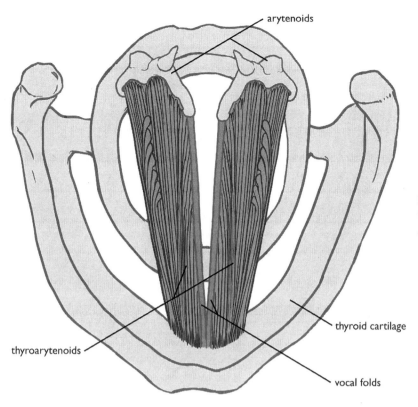

Figure 3.4 Action of the thyroarytenoids. *Sandy Escobar.*

arytenoids

thyroid cartilage

thyroarytenoids

vocal folds

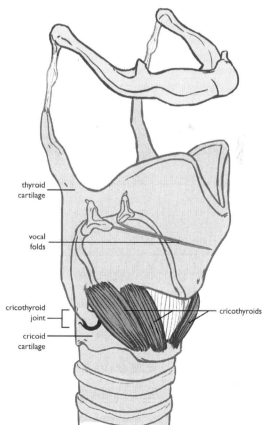

Figure 3.5 Cricothyroids. *Sandy Escobar.*

thyroid cartilage

vocal folds

cricothyroid joint

cricoid cartilage

cricothyroids

The Cricothyroids

Figure 3.6 shows the action of the cricothyroid muscles, which is a little more difficult to visualize than the action of the thyroarytenoids because the cricothyroids are not attached to the vocal folds and can only influence their length and thickness indirectly. The cricothyroids originate on the front and sides of the cricoid cartilage and attach at an angle to the thyroid cartilage. When they contract, they rotate the thyroid cartilage forward at the cricothyroid joints, as shown in figure 3.6. This increases the distance between the vocal folds' points of attachment to the thyroid cartilage and the arytenoid cartilages, causing the vocal folds to elongate and narrow, raising pitch and lightening registration.

An Agonist/Antagonist Relationship

The combined activity of the thyroarytenoid and cricothyroid muscles varies the length and thickness of the vocal folds, modulating pitch and registration.

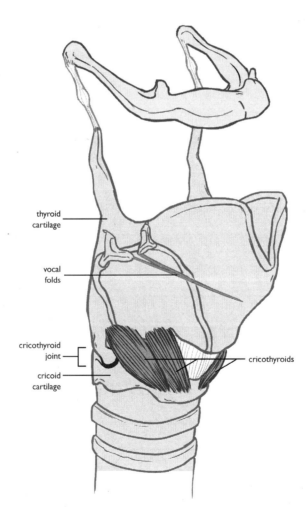

Figure 3.6 Action of the cricothyroids. *Sandy Escobar.*

Muscle groups function in tandem to generate and stabilize movement around each joint in the body and throughout the skeletomuscular system. For example, the hamstrings and quadriceps work together to produce knee movement. Your hamstrings are the major muscles located in the back of your thigh, between your knee and buttocks, while the quadriceps are the major muscles in the front. When your hamstrings contract and your quadriceps lengthen, this action serves to bend, or flex, your knee; when your quadriceps contract and your hamstrings lengthen, this produces the opposite effect on the knee, causing it to straighten, or extend. The hamstrings and quadriceps collaborate to control the rate of movement and degree of force production around your knee. This partnership between such opposing muscle groups is called an agonist/antagonist relationship. Bend your knee in a variety of positions and at different speeds, and observe its movement when walking or running. Because you have a great deal of experience flexing and extending your knees, these movements are smooth and easy for you to control.

Your thyroarytenoid and cricothyroid muscles share a partnership similar to the one between your hamstrings and quadriceps. The thyroarytenoids create thickness by shortening and thickening the vocal folds, while the cricothyroids oppose their movements to create narrowness and length. Together, they are capable of changing the length and thickness of your vocal folds in a way that can potentially yield smooth, stable, and balanced movement.

Laryngeal Mobility and Stabilization

The larynx as a whole enjoys exceptional mobility because it has very few attachments to other structures; most of the structures to which it is attached are themselves fairly flexible. The larynx is suspended from the hyoid bone, which does not connect directly to any other bones; from below, the larynx is attached to the trachea by the cricotracheal ligament, which is also a relatively pliable structure. The stability of the larynx therefore depends upon balancing and coordinating the muscles capable of elevating and depressing it.

The Laryngeal Elevators

The laryngeal elevators include the digastric, stylohyoid, mylohyoid, and geniohyoid muscles, shown in figure 3.7. Their primary function is facilitating swallowing, an activity upon which our survival depends. Given the significance our laryngeal elevators hold for our well-being, it is understandable that they evolved to become quite strong—notably stronger, as it turns out, than our laryngeal depressors.

The Laryngeal Depressors

The laryngeal depressors include the sternohyoid, sternothyroid, thyrohyoid, and omohyoid, shown in figure 3.8. Their primary function is to stabilize the hyoid bone and larynx by serving as antagonists to the laryngeal elevators.

Classical voice teachers advocate cultivating a low laryngeal position because so doing will maximize the length of the supraglottal tract, optimize resonance, and facilitate good range of motion at the cricothyroid joints. As the laryngeal elevators are more numerous and stronger than the laryngeal depressors, a low laryngeal position is best achieved by alleviating tightness and overactivity in the laryngeal elevators rather than engaging the laryngeal depressors in an attempt to override this tightness and overactivity.

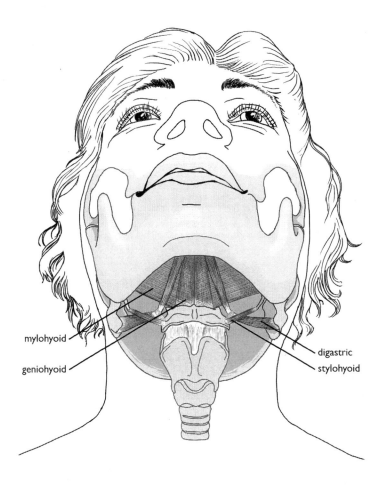

mylohyoid

geniohyoid

digastric

stylohyoid

Figure 3.7 Laryngeal elevators. *Sandy Escobar.*

Laryngeal Range of Motion

How high and how low you can sing is determined in part by genetics and in part by the range of motion you are able to access at the cricothyroid joints—the degree to which your cricothyroid muscles are able to tilt the thyroid cartilage forward and consequently lengthen your vocal folds. Optimizing range of motion at the cricothyroid joints is therefore key to extending your range upward. However, if you wish to optimize laryngeal range of motion, you may need to do more than just strengthen your cricothyroid muscles.

In addition to cricothyroid function, there are numerous factors that impact range of motion at the cricothyroid joints. Chief among them are the structures surrounding the larynx. Laryngeal movement is obstructed when it bumps into something unyielding, so all of the structures that attach to and surround your larynx must be well conditioned and coordinated for your larynx to enjoy the fullest possible range of motion.

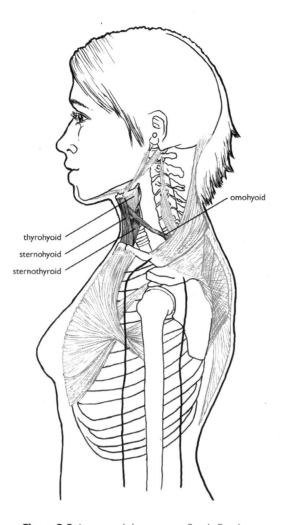

Figure labels: omohyoid, thyrohyoid, sternohyoid, sternothyroid

Figure 3.8 Laryngeal depressors. *Sandy Escobar.*

Assessing Laryngeal Range of Motion

This assessment will enable you to troubleshoot for some of the issues that can limit laryngeal range of motion and identify specific areas in need of improved flexibility and coordination.

1. With your voice well warmed up, perform a slow siren on [ɑ] (ah as in "papa") that traverses your entire range, ascending and descending, without breaking into falsetto.

    •   Note the lowest and highest pitches.

2. Place one hand high on your chest and your other hand high on your abdomen.

    •   Repeat the siren, starting on the same low note but ascending only as high as you can without increasing engagement in your abdominal muscles or depressing your sternum.

    •   Note the top pitch.

3. Allow your jaw to relax and observe yourself in a mirror.

   - Repeat the siren, ascending only as high as you can without opening your jaw any farther or spreading your lips sideways.

   - Note the top pitch.

4. Allow your jaw to relax and gently press a thumb against the underside of your chin where your jaw meets your neck.

   - Repeat the siren, ascending only as high as you can without feeling the area under your thumb stiffen and retract.

   - Note the top pitch.

5. Compare the results of your initial siren with the subsequent three.

If you were capable of reaching a higher (or even a much higher) pitch on your initial siren than you were on one or all of those that followed, this indicates the presence of tensions that are impeding your laryngeal range of motion. The fact that you can access a given high note, even when it involves overriding some tension, suggests that you can become capable of tuning that note with greater freedom and less effort once the interfering tension has been identified and alleviated.

- An increase in abdominal engagement or depressing the sternum indicates an instinct to increase subglottal breath pressure in order to override whatever resistance may be impeding laryngeal range of motion. The first step in identifying the nature of this resistance is inhibiting the instinct to override it. If you are able to refrain from increasing your subglottal breath pressure, you may be able to detect what is creating the resistance and take steps to alleviate it.

- A tendency to open the jaw wide or spread the lips sideways as the pitch ascends indicates a larynx that is ascending along with the pitch and/or inadequate internal vowel height. Relaxing the laryngeal elevators, optimizing alignment of the cervical spine, and improving articulatory efficiency can facilitate a lower laryngeal position.

- A stiffening of the underside of the chin indicates an increase in tension in the base of the tongue (the hyoglossus) and/or the mylohyoid, one of the laryngeal elevators. As both of these muscles are connected to the hyoid bone, from which the larynx is suspended, overactivity in this area will compromise laryngeal mobility.

Three key ways to maximize laryngeal range of motion are relaxing the laryngeal elevators, optimizing alignment of the cervical spine, and improving articulatory efficiency.

RELAXING THE LARYNGEAL ELEVATORS

As mentioned above, there are advantages to maintaining a low laryngeal position. A low laryngeal position facilitates good range of motion at the cricothyroid joints; it also indicates a lack of tension and overactivity in the laryngeal elevators. Conversely, the higher the larynx, the greater the potential for surrounding structures to crowd it and impede its range of motion.

The best strategy for maintaining a low larynx is to refrain from elevating it in the first place, so it is important to learn to relax the laryngeal elevators, particularly the digastric muscle. The digastric attaches the hyoid bone to the jaw in the front and the skull in the back, as shown in figure 3.10, so it is ideally positioned to hoist the larynx up. Tightness and overactivity in the digastric muscle can be effectively alleviated through massage.

MASSAGE FOR THE DIGASTRIC MUSCLE

- Using your fingers or a handheld massager, massage the muscles at the very top of your spine and just below your skull on both sides, as shown in figure 3.9. While massaging this area, slowly draw your chin toward your chest and then return your neck to an upright position as though nodding "yes" several times.

- While maintaining a long, relaxed position of your neck, massage the underside of your jawline, beginning at the sides and working toward the center of your chin.

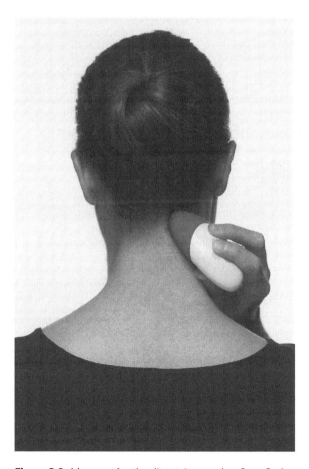

Figure 3.9 Massage for the digastric muscles. *Ryan Parker.*

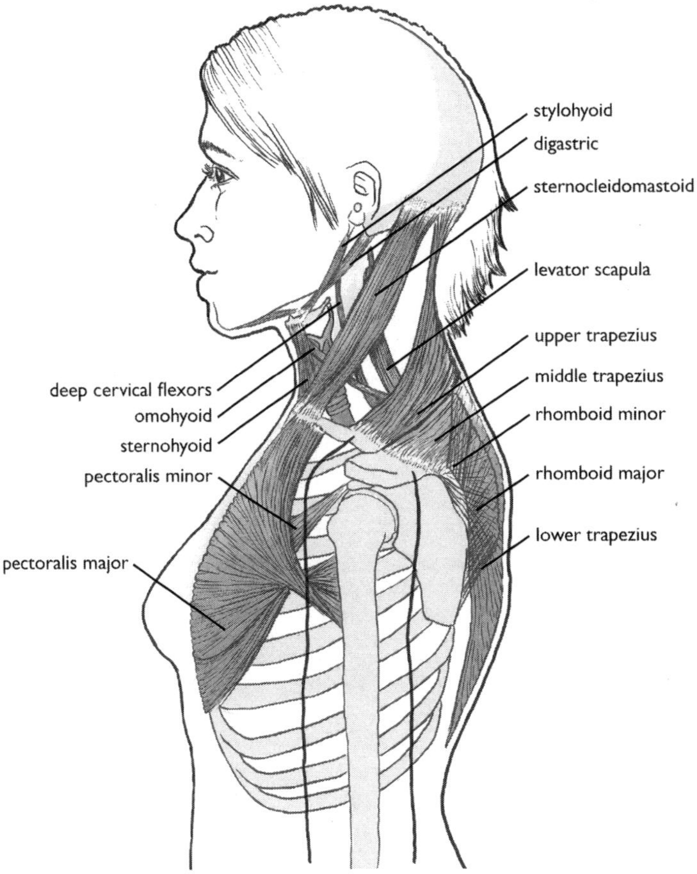
stylohyoid
digastric
sternocleidomastoid
levator scapula
upper trapezius
middle trapezius
rhomboid minor
rhomboid major
lower trapezius
deep cervical flexors
omohyoid
sternohyoid
pectoralis minor
pectoralis major

Figure 3.10 Laryngeal position in healthy upper-body alignment. *Sandy Escobar.*

- When both areas feel free of tension, resume massaging the muscles in the back of your neck while performing ascending and descending scales or arpeggios, encouraging your neck muscles to remain relaxed on the ascent.

ALIGNMENT OF THE CERVICAL SPINE

As discussed in chapter 1, a very common postural distortion is an exaggerated curve of the neck, often resulting in a forward position of the head. This exaggerated curve distorts and compresses the space inside the throat and is likely to limit range of motion for the larynx.

Note the orientation of the larynx within the throat shown in figure 3.10 in comparison with its position in figure 3.11, and you will appreciate how vital good alignment is for optimal vocal function. The muscular imbalances characteristic of upper crossed syndrome change the default angle of the neck, impacting the position of all of the structures housed within it. A fitness regimen targeting upper crossed syndrome can restore the upper body to alignment more favorable to laryngeal freedom.

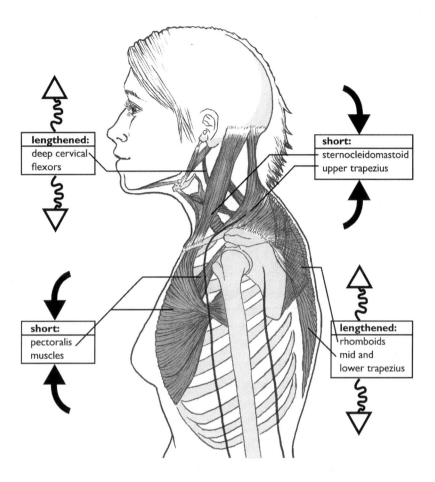

lengthened:
deep cervical
flexors

short:
sternocleidomastoid
upper trapezius

short:
pectoralis
muscles

lengthened:
rhomboids
mid and
lower trapezius

Figure 3.11 Laryngeal position in upper crossed syndrome. *Sandy Escobar.*

Optimizing Alignment of the Cervical Spine

If your results from the assessments you performed in chapter 1 indicate upper crossed syndrome, this sequence of exercises drawn from chapter 6 will help improve the alignment of your cervical spine:

- self-myofascial release for the shoulders

- self-myofascial release for the latissumus dorsi

- static stretch for the pectoral muscles

- static stretch for the latissimus dorsi

- half-angel shoulder stretch

- single leg scaption

- lat pulldown

Keep in mind that while these exercises will help restore balance to the cervical spine, it is important to incorporate this sequence into a comprehensive whole-body fitness regimen, as anything that impacts the upper body will have an effect throughout the entire skeletomuscular system.

ARTICULATORY EFFICIENCY

Poor articulatory coordination can impinge on laryngeal movement in a variety of ways. Retracting the tongue in order to stabilize or lower the larynx creates tension that can limit laryngeal mobility. A jaw that is held too closed or too open may distort what little internal space is available, not only for laryngeal movement but also for resonance and articulation. Inadequate expansion and vowel "height" within the oropharynx, especially on higher pitches, can lead to a compensatory elevation of the larynx and a sideways spread of the lips. Strategies for improving flexibility and coordination of the tongue, jaw, and other articulators will be covered in chapter 4.

If you experience an increased sense of effort as you approach the top of your range, it is likely that your larynx is meeting resistance as it strives to move into the proper position to tune higher pitches. Rather than exert extra effort to overcome this resistance, troubleshoot for these common problems that can impede laryngeal range of motion and take steps to alleviate them.

Vocal Registration

The thyroarytenoid and cricothyroid muscles work together to tune the vocal folds to a desired pitch by adjusting their length; in addition, these two muscles collaborate to modulate the weight of registration by adjusting vocal fold thickness.

The concept of distinct registers arose during the bel canto period. Many voice teachers continue to describe heavy vocal production as "chest voice" and light vocal production as "head voice." While our anatomical understanding of registration remains incomplete as of this writing, it has become clear to voice scientists that the traditional terminology does not precisely align with actual vocal fold function. Pedagogues now prefer the terms "TA dominant" and "CT dominant" to describe ranges of heavy and light registration as a means of indicating whether the thyroarytenoid muscles or the cricothyroid muscles are exerting greater influence over vocal production. But given the awkwardness of such language, it is not surprising that the traditional terminology persists.

I believe that the reason it is so intuitive to conceive of the voice as divided into two registers stems from the way our voice use generally develops. We engage the voice in spoken communication for many years prior to studying singing technique, favoring the low range and heavy production that is the province of the thyroarytenoids. Thus, when we begin to explore the high range that is the province of the cricothyroids, we find these muscles to be far less developed and coordinated than the thyroarytenoids and that a balanced agonist/antagonist relationship has yet to be developed. In the absence of such a balance, it will seem that we must choose to allow one or the other of these muscles to dominate on a given pitch, deliberately develop chest voice and head voice separately, and then seek to blend them together to avoid developing a "hole" in the middle of the range.

I find it both more practical and anatomically correct to conceive of registration as a continuum rather than as a dichotomy and to view the vocal folds as capable of seamlessly evolving from thick to thin and back, just as they are capable of seamlessly evolving from low to high and back. It is possible to cultivate a balanced agonist/antagonist relationship between the thyroarytenoids and cricothyroids, and once this has been established the distinctions between clearly defined registers will fade or disappear entirely.

Equalizing Registration

Vocal exercises employing sirens and scales traversing a wide range facilitate good cooperation between the muscles governing registration. In particular, descending sirens and scales help condition the cricothyroids, which will likely remain at a disadvantage throughout our lives due to the amount of time we continually devote to thyroarytenoid-dominated speech.

Here are some exercises for developing balance between the muscles of registration. Perform them with a simple, steady release of your breath, keeping your throat as relaxed as possible.

DESCENDING SIRENS

Starting on a high pitch you can easily access with what you would consider your head voice, perform a slow descending siren to the bottom of your range. Use any vowel you prefer.

- Are you able to siren all the way down with consistent quality and focus, or are there sudden changes in the weight and timbre of your voice?

- Is your siren continuous from top to bottom, or does your voice skip out for an interval on the way down?

At the onset of a descending siren, your cricothyroids dominate the quality of registration. As you descend, your thyroarytenoids ideally become gradually more active in order to modulate pitch and registration while maintaining consistent timbre.

- If when you arrive at the bottom of the siren you find that your tone is relatively weak or diffuse, this may be due to inadequate engagement of the thyroarytenoids. Encourage weightier registration sooner as you descend, even if at first you are not able to transition smoothly.

- If your voice suddenly breaks into heavier registration on the descent, you may be allowing the thyroarytenoids to suddenly take over rather than maintaining continuous engagement of the cricothyroids while allowing an increase in thyroarytenoid engagement. Try performing descending sirens while maintaining lighter registration lower into the descent; allow for a break if necessary, but encourage it to occur later and lower.

ASCENDING SIRENS

Starting toward the bottom of your range with a quality of registration you would associate with chest voice, perform a slow ascending siren as high as you comfortably can. Use any vowel you prefer.

- Is it easy for you to ascend into what you would consider head-voice range, or is there an increased sense of strain as you move into and above the passaggio?

- Are you able to siren up with consistent quality, focus, and comfort, or are there sudden changes in the weight, timbre, and freedom of your voice?

- Is the siren continuous from bottom to top, or does your voice skip out for an interval on the way up?

At the onset of an ascending siren that starts low, your thyroarytenoids dominate the quality of registration. As you ascend, your thyroarytenoids become gradually less active while the cricothyroids become more active in order to modulate pitch and registration while maintaining consistent timbre.

- If you find that your throat tightens as you ascend and that you cannot move comfortably into and above the passaggio, it may mean that your thyroarytenoids are maintaining constant tension rather than gradually ceding control to the cricothyroids. Encourage lighter registration lower in the ascent even if at first you are not able to transition to it smoothly.

- If your voice suddenly breaks into lighter registration and/or skips an interval on the ascent, this may indicate a need to engage your cricothyroids more actively at the beginning of the siren so they partner well with the thyroarytenoids throughout. Allow the overall registration to become lighter lower in the ascent; allow any break or sudden shift to occur earlier.

While singers may instinctively strive to avoid the startling sound and sensation of a break in the voice, eliciting a "crack" in both directions is a useful way to explore the registration continuum and to equalize strength between the muscles that govern registration. The bel canto masters who first codified the vocal registers, as well as modern voice scientists, agree that exposing registration imbalances is an essential step on the path to resolving them.

Almost any note you sing is not restricted to a specific optimal weight but can rather be produced within a range of heaviness or lightness, depending upon the musical style, desired expressive color or dynamic level, whether it is approached from above or below, and other factors. Develop balanced strength and coordination between your muscles of registration, and you will enjoy not only seamless continuity of timbre from top to bottom but also a wide variety of expressive possibilities throughout your range.

When I first meet with a fitness client who is new to strength training, they often have misgivings about their ability to realize their goals. However, while they may find it difficult to imagine achieving the improvements they desire for their alignment, strength, and stamina, I have great confidence that they can, if they consistently follow the regimen I design for them. I believe that it is possible for voice teachers to offer a similar degree of confidence when working with students who struggle to access their full range or sing with even registration. Just as trainers address their

Complete Vocal Fitness

clients' alignment issues and muscular imbalances prior to pursuing major strength and performance goals, we can devise a pedagogical approach that addresses muscular imbalances in and around the larynx and optimizes laryngeal range of motion prior to focusing on sound production as an end in itself.

Absent any medical issues, your vocal folds can be trained to produce a focused sound, vibrate freely throughout your entire pitch range, modulate registration seamlessly, and express an organic vibrato rather than the exaggerations characteristic of a bleat or a wobble. An inability to do any of these things is not due to any built-in limitation of your voice, any more than would be true of a cyclist whose left leg is stronger than the right. We have techniques at our disposal to help the cyclist develop strength in the right leg, and we also have techniques to help singers develop balanced strength between the thyroarytenoid and cricothyroid muscles. It may require consistent, focused practice over a period of time, but this balance can be achieved.

4

Articulation

Classical ballet classes commence with a traditional structure: a period of stretching, followed by practice of the five fundamental foot positions. All five positions require a turnout from the hip and precise alignment of the hips, knees, and ankles. These positions are integral to every barre exercise and movement combination that will follow, so it is vital to habituate and reinforce them prior to performing more complicated movements (see figure 4.1).

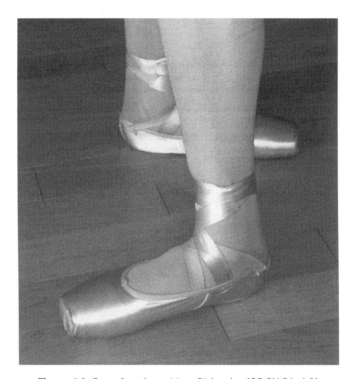

Figure 4.1 Open fourth position. *Richwales (CC-BY-SA-4.0).*

Symbols appearing in brackets are drawn from the International Phonetic Alphabet. IPA is the pronunciation guide in common use by classical singers that notates the sounds of language.

While ballet dancers are restricted to these five foot positions during training and performance, once they leave the studio or theater they resume using their legs more or less the same ways as nondancers do. You may notice the impact of a dancer's training on their overall bearing, but you will not observe them turning out from the hip as they walk down the street, navigate stairs, drive a car, and so on. Dancers need their legs to accomplish a wide variety of movements and tasks that are unrelated to dancing, just as singers use the assorted components of their vocal anatomy to do things like carry on a conversation, consume a meal, and engage in physical exercise.

The continual reinforcement of the five foot positions at the beginning of ballet class provides dancers the opportunity to rehabituate their legs to the positions and movements that will enable them to dance well and facilitates a transition from habitual, utilitarian leg use to that narrower range of body language through which they express themselves as they dance.

Where articulation is concerned, singers would greatly benefit from an equivalent opportunity. We need a ballet class for our mouths—a structured means of rehabituating our jaws, tongues, lips, and soft palates to positions that provide for optimal lyric diction, supplanting our speech habits with elegant, well-coordinated movements capable of defining clean, intelligible sung phonemes.

Habitual versus Optimal Articulation

The supraglottal tract, comprising the pharynx and the oral and nasal cavities, is the resonator for the vocal instrument. This highly malleable space amplifies vocal fold vibration and is capable of molding it into a wide variety of tone colors. As articulation and resonance are functionally intertwined, it is useful to view articulation as a component of resonance.

Optimal vocal resonance is defined by the ability to shape the supraglottal tract in a way that consistently amplifies the vibrations produced by the vocal folds as we move from vowel to vowel and pitch to pitch. Optimal articulation, therefore, requires the ability to shape vowels and consonants so as to provide for this consistent amplification.

The way we learn to articulate vowels and consonants in speech rarely provides for optimal vocal resonance.

We learn speech by imitating the sounds and articulatory movements of those around us, and our aim is intelligible expression rather than consistent, powerful resonance. While the way we naturally articulate some phonemes will prove more useful for lyric diction than others, optimizing articulation for singing generally demands a wholesale reeducation of the jaw, tongue, lips, and soft palate.

I will first discuss the articulators individually, describing their structure and movements and offering means to assess and improve their function. Then I will share some exercises for coordinating them together to facilitate optimal intelligibility and resonance while singing.

The Jaw

The jaw comprises a pair of bones: the upper jaw, or maxilla, and the lower jaw, or mandible, shown in figure 4.2. The maxilla is fused with its neighboring skull bones and does not move. The mandible is attached to the skull at the temporomandibular joints.

The temporomandibular joints are highly versatile and unstable, enabling the mandible to move up and down, forward and back, and side to side. I will restrict my discussion to those jaw movements that are useful for singing articulation: rotation and translation.

Figure 4.3 shows the position of the mandible when the jaw is closed. The movement of the mandible when you begin to open your mouth is called rotation, shown in figure 4.4. The mandible

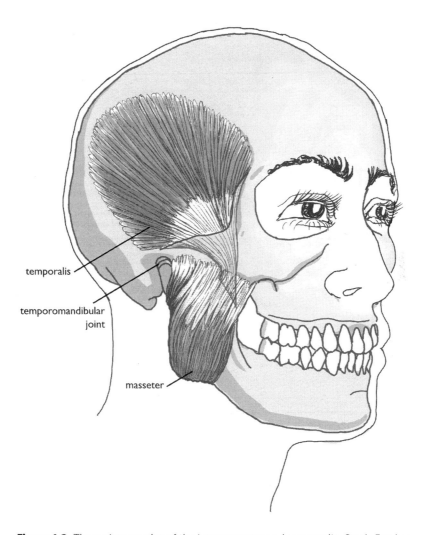

Figure 4.2 The major muscles of the jaw: masseter and temporalis. *Sandy Escobar.*

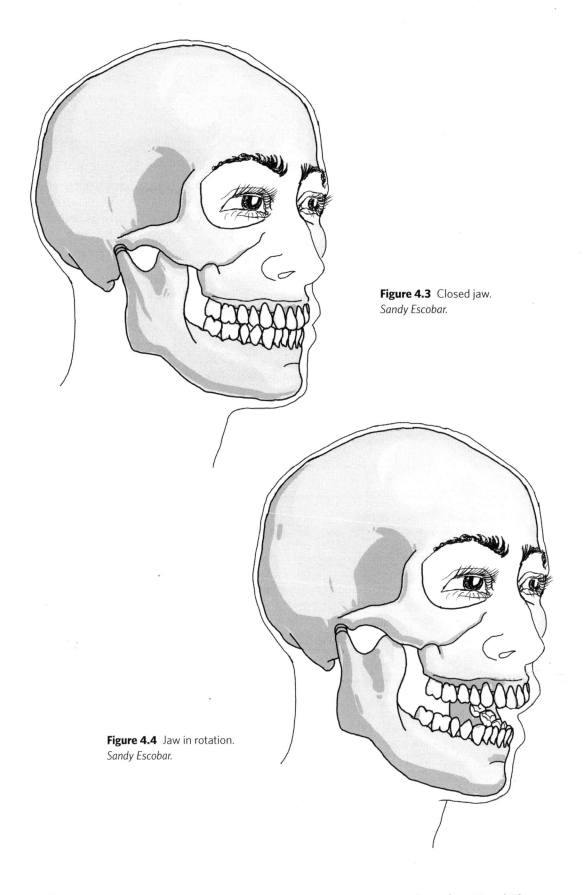

Figure 4.3 Closed jaw.
Sandy Escobar.

Figure 4.4 Jaw in rotation.
Sandy Escobar.

swivels down like a hinge, yielding one to two fingers' width of space between the upper and lower front teeth. As your mouth opens wider, the mandible goes into translation, shown in figure 4.5. As the mandible continues to lower, it also slides forward. Place your hands on either side of your face as you slowly open your jaw wide, and you will be able to detect the moment when the mandible moves from rotation into translation.

The two main muscles governing jaw movement are the masseter and the temporalis, shown in figure 4.2; the primary function for both is mastication. The masseter is the strongest muscle in the body based on weight. When you consider that our hunter-gatherer ancestors once had to chew uncooked vegetables and meat, you can appreciate that these muscles are far more powerful than is required for any of the movements we perform while singing.

The muscles of the jaw therefore have a tendency to be overactive and tight. To optimize the masseter and temporalis for singing, we must release and stretch them.

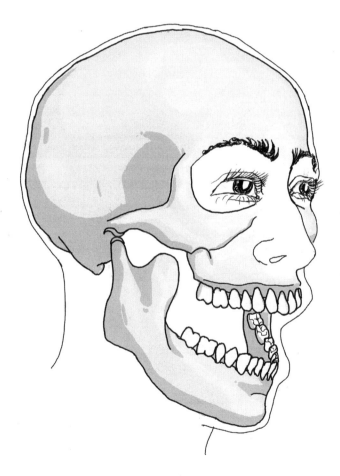

Figure 4.5 Jaw in translation. *Sandy Escobar.*

RELEASE THE JAW MUSCLES

Locate the masseter by placing your hands on either side of your face and noting where you feel a bulge when pressing your teeth together. Gently massage your masseter using your fingertips or a small massager, as shown in figure 4.6. Begin with the jaw closed and then slowly open and close the jaw while continuing the massage. Repeat this movement several times, noting whether the jaw is tighter on one side than the other and whether the movement is smooth or irregular.

Locate the temporalis by feeling for an indentation on either side of your skull just above and to the sides of your eyebrows. Gently massage your temporalis using your fingertips or a small massager. Begin with the jaw closed and then slowly open and close the jaw while continuing the massage. Repeat this movement several times, noting whether the jaw is tighter on one side than the other and whether the movement is smooth or irregular.

STRETCH THE JAW MUSCLES

Relax your neck and establish good upper-body alignment. Open your jaw and place the index and middle fingers of both hands over your lower teeth toward the sides. Open your jaw as wide as you comfortably can and then exert a gentle downward pull with your fingers. Continue to breathe. Hold the stretch for a minimum of thirty seconds.

Figure 4.6 Massage for the jaw. *Ryan Parker.*

The Tongue

The tongue is a highly malleable organ composed primarily of muscle tissue. Its movements are controlled primarily by means of four pairs of extrinsic muscles: the genioglossus, the hyoglossus, the styloglossus, and the palatoglossus, shown in figure 4.7.

The tongue is among the most effective multitaskers in the human body; it is responsible for tasting and swallowing food, verbal articulation, and keeping teeth clean. The tongue's singing tasks include the definition of vowels by adjusting its height within the oral cavity and the formation of consonants by articulating against the teeth and various positions of the hard palate.

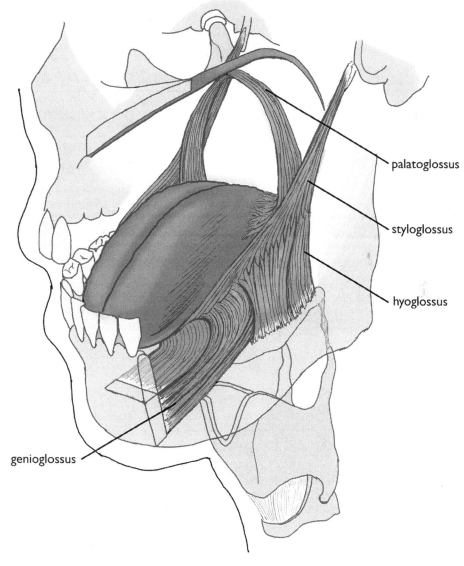

Figure 4.7 Extrinsic muscles of the tongue. *Sandy Escobar.*

The genioglossus and hyoglossus, shown in figures 4.8 and 4.9, are the tongue muscles that most require optimization and coordination for singing articulation.

The genioglossus protrudes the tongue, as shown in figure 4.8. It is responsible for moving the tip or middle of the tongue into position for articulating dental and palatal consonants, among many other things.

The hyoglossus originates in the hyoid bone, from which the larynx is suspended; it retracts and depresses the tongue, as shown in figure 4.9. When singers complain of tongue tension, what they are

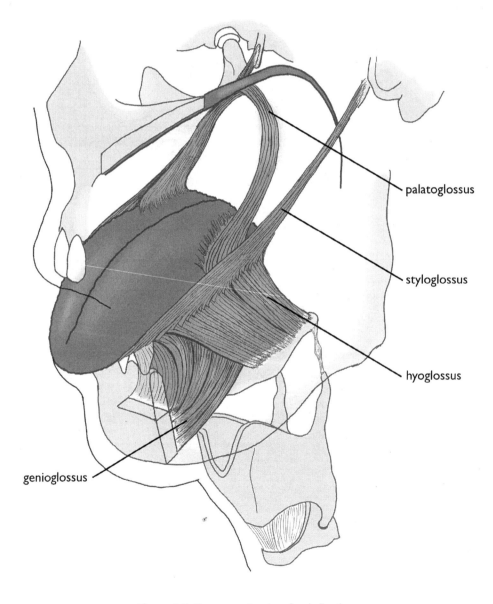

Figure 4.8 Tongue protrusion. *Sandy Escobar.*

likely referring to is the action of the hyoglossus retracting and depressing the base of the tongue. This movement compresses the distance between the tongue and the hyoid bone, impeding the mobility of the laryngeal cartilages by constricting the area within which they are able to move.

You can monitor for a tight or overactive hyoglossus by gently pressing a thumb against the underside of your chin toward your throat. Massage this area lightly until it feels soft and relaxed; then perform some simple vocal exercises while continuing to monitor with your thumb. If you feel this area stiffen, press down against your thumb or shake in tandem with your vibrato. An overactive hyoglossus is retracting your tongue as you sing.

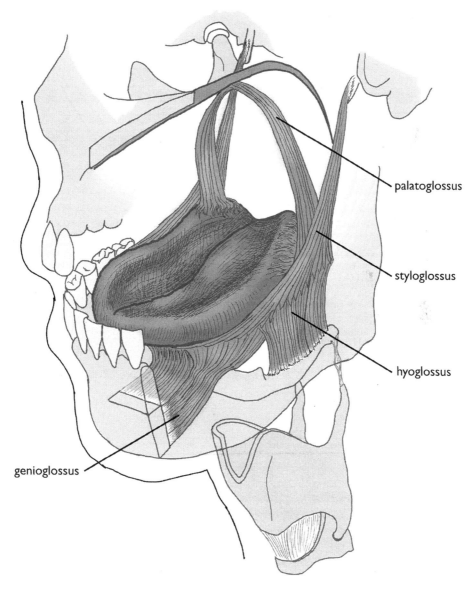

Figure 4.9 Tongue retraction. *Sandy Escobar.*

While I appreciate that there are voice teachers who advocate for a retracted or "grooved" tongue, a majority recommend keeping tongue retraction to a minimum; in addition, the illustrations of tongue positions for vowel definition that appear in diction texts universally depict a range of arched positions that cannot be achieved with a retracted tongue. However, it is not my intention to promote a particular tongue position but rather to facilitate optimal tongue coordination so that you can do with it what you intend rather than allow it to be controlled by chronic tensions or unconscious habits.

The genioglossus and the hyoglossus have an agonist/antagonist relationship. The hyoglossus tends to be overactive and tight, resulting in a weak and underactive genioglossus. To optimize the muscles of the tongue for singing, we must release and stretch the hyoglossus and strengthen the genioglossus.

Release the hyoglossus. Gently massage the underside of your chin using your fingertips or a small massager, as shown in figure 4.10. Maintain a long, relaxed position with your neck. Moving slowly, stick your tongue out as far as you can and then draw it back into your mouth. Repeat this movement several times, noting whether the movement is smooth or irregular.

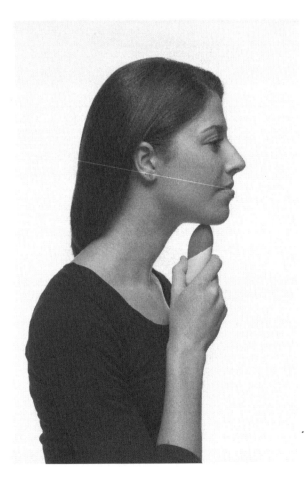

Figure 4.10 Massage for the tongue. *Ryan Parker.*

Stretch the hyoglossus. Relax your neck and establish good upper-body alignment. Wrap the tip of your tongue in a piece of gauze or a paper towel, holding it in place with the fingers of both hands. Stick your tongue out as far as you can, then gently pull on it with your fingers. Continue to breathe. Hold the stretch for a minimum of thirty seconds.

Strengthen the genioglossus. Place a long, slender object such as a wooden pencil or crochet hook underneath your tongue and hold it in place by pressing the tip of your tongue against the back of your lower front teeth. Perform some short scales or arpeggios while defining the best [ɑ] (ah) vowel you can in this position, continuing to press your tongue against your lower teeth. Be patient and persistent if your tongue habitually retracts when you begin to vocalize or shortly thereafter, adjusting the exercise to a shorter duration and/or narrower range as needed.

The Lips

The lips surround the oral cavity on all sides. The muscles that act on the lips include the buccinator, orbicularis oris, and zygomaticus major, shown in figure 4.11, all of which are considered muscles of facial expression.

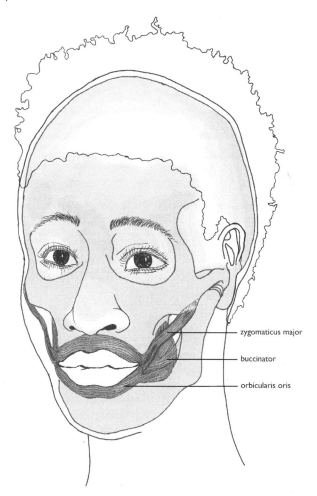

Figure 4.11 Articulatory muscles of the lips. *Sandy Escobar.*

The orbicularis oris rounds the lips as shown in figure 4.12 and is capable of varying the degree of rounding at any point around its circumference. The zygomaticus major, known as one of the "smile muscles," draws the corners of the lips out toward the sides, as shown in figure 4.13. The buccinator draws the cheeks in toward the teeth, assisting with such movements as sucking, whistling, and smiling.

The lip muscle most important for singing articulation is the orbicularis oris. We tend to underutilize this muscle in everyday speech when defining vowels such as [ɔ] (aw as in "saw"), [o] (oh as in "home") and [u] (oo as in "moon"), as we can produce these vowels intelligibly by altering the

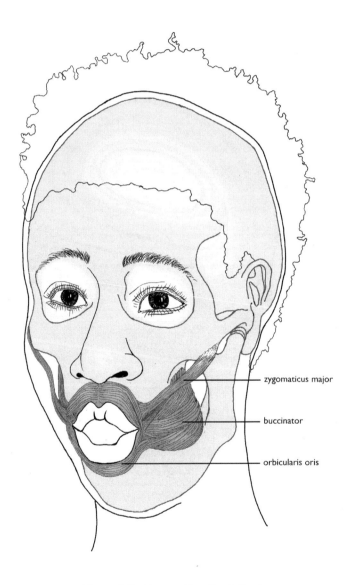

zygomaticus major

buccinator

orbicularis oris

Figure 4.12 Lip rounding. *Sandy Escobar.*

shape of the tongue. However, defining these vowels by rounding the lips affords optimal resonance, whereas producing them with the tongue may interfere with the mobility of the larynx.

The zygomaticus major is responsible for a lateral spread of the lips that can interfere with resonance. In speech we tend to engage this muscle when articulating [i] (ee as in "seem"), [ɛ] (eh as in "head") and related vowel sounds, so it is important to retrain our mouths to define these vowels with the tongue while allowing the lips to remain relaxed. If the technique you practice advocates engaging the "smile muscles," be sure that you are doing so with intention and not as the result of chronic tensions or speech habits.

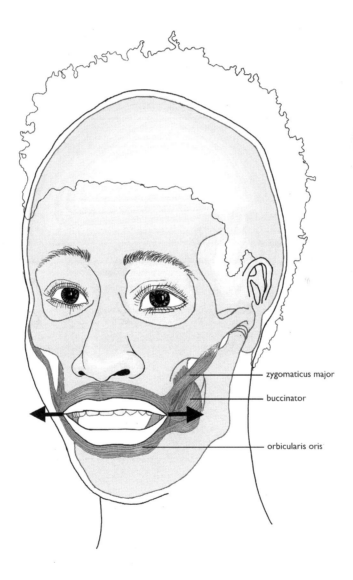

zygomaticus major

buccinator

orbicularis oris

Figure 4.13 Lateral spread of the lips. *Sandy Escobar.*

The buccinator can act as an articulatory synergist for either the orbicularis oris or the zygomaticus major. It can assist with rounding and draw the lips inward, as in whistling or forming a trumpet embouchure; alternately, it can draw the cheeks inward and out to the sides, as in smiling, and is the muscle responsible for the formation of dimples.

The zygomaticus major has a tendency to be overactive, while the orbicularis oris tends to be underactive. To optimize the lip muscles for singing, we must release the zygomaticus major, strengthen the orbicularis oris, and encourage the buccinators to partner effectively with the orbicularis oris rather than contribute to the spread that can be so problematic for resonance. Due to the interdependent nature of these three muscles, they are most effectively trained in combination rather than in isolation.

Release the zygomaticus major and buccinators. Firmly massage your checks on either side of your jaw using your fingertips or a small massager. Maintain a long, relaxed position of your neck and open the jaw into rotation position. Moving slowly, round your lips and then stretch them laterally in an exaggerated smile, while allowing the jaw to remain open and relaxed. Repeat this movement several times, noting whether the movement is smooth or irregular.

Engage the orbicularis oris and buccinators. Place the soft underside of your palm just below the thumb between your lips. Engage the orbicularis oris to form a seal around the area and then engage the buccinator by beginning to suck steadily, sustaining this movement for four to eight seconds and then relaxing. Repeat three to five times.

Coordinate the lip muscles. While observing your face in a mirror, use a sustained speaking voice to slowly alternate between the vowel sounds [ɑ] and [o] by moving your lips from a relaxed to a rounded position and back again. Allow your jaw to remain completely still throughout and repeat the movement several times. When this becomes comfortable and well coordinated, perform a siren from the bottom of your range to the top and back again, beginning on [ɑ] and gradually morphing to [o] as the pitch ascends. Rather than rounding on the way up your lips, try to spread sideways and massage your cheeks as you perform the exercise to encourage relaxation of the zygomaticus major. Perform the siren only as high as you can while inhibiting a sideways spread.

The Soft Palate

The soft palate, shown in figure 4.14, makes up the rear portion of the roof of the mouth. Located behind the hard palate, the soft palate is composed of muscle and connective tissue, surrounded by mucous membrane. It is capable of elevating, lowering, and tensing laterally.

The soft palate elevates to close the nasal port during swallowing to prevent food from entering the nasal cavity. In speech, it interacts with the back of the tongue to articulate velar consonants, including [ŋ] (ng as in "hung"), [k], and [g]. It contributes to vocal resonance by regulating nasality.

When the soft palate is in a relaxed position, as shown in figure 4.15, the nasal port is open, permitting air to move in and out through both the nose and the mouth. When the soft palate is in a raised position, as shown in figure 4.16, it closes the nasal port such that air can move in and out only through the mouth.

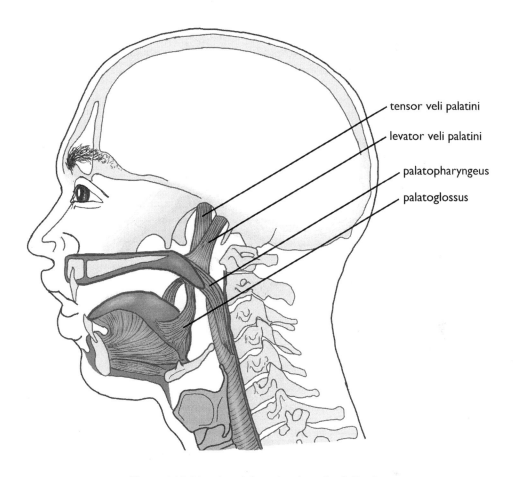

Figure 4.14 Muscles of the soft palate. *Sandy Escobar.*

A majority of classical voice teachers recommend a raised position of the soft palate for achieving full and balanced resonance while singing; there are others who advocate a relaxed soft palate. Either way, it is important to understand how this articulator works in order to ensure that it is doing what you want it to do.

Two muscles contribute to soft-palate elevation: the levator veli palatini and tensor veli palatini, shown in figure 4.14. These muscles attach the soft palate to positions inside the skull and do not directly interact with any other muscles, such as those located in the cheeks or forehead. The palatoglossus attaches to the tongue and pulls the palate closer to the tongue rather than lifts it. The palatopharyngeus attaches to the thyroid cartilage of the larynx and causes not the soft palate but rather the larynx to slightly ascend in support of swallowing.

We have very little direct control over the soft palate and receive little sensory feedback from its movements. As a result, many myths and misconceptions have arisen regarding the engagement of the soft palate in singing. I have offered such detail in describing the muscles of the soft palate in the hope of clarifying some misconceptions:

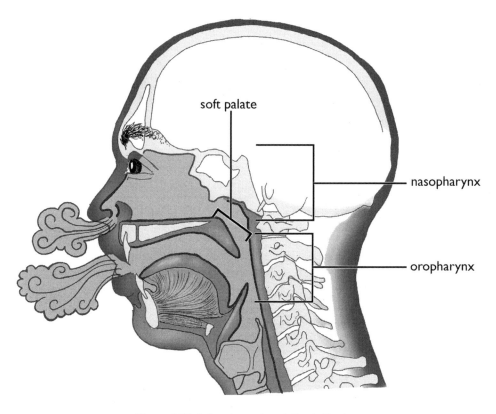

Figure 4.15 Soft palate relaxed. *Sandy Escobar.*

Raising the soft palate does not cause the tongue to depress. The soft palate is connected to the tongue via the palatoglossus; when this muscle is engaged, the soft palate and tongue will raise and lower in tandem.

Tensing your forehead to raise your eyebrows does not elevate the soft palate; neither will elevating your lips in a sneer. None of the facial muscles have any connection to the soft palate; the muscles that raise the soft palate are attached to the skull.

The soft palate does not lift and expand like a parachute in response to breath release. The sensation of airflow moving across the soft palate when it is in a raised position may make it feel as though there is a causal connection, but this is not the case.

Given how little sensation we experience in the soft palate, the best way to become familiar with how it moves is through direct observation. Have a look inside your mouth with a mirror or phone camera (putting your camera in video mode with the flash turned on works well). When your soft palate is relaxed, you will see the uvula dangling in the center from the back of the roof of your mouth. The soft palate is the mobile muscular structure from which the uvula is suspended.

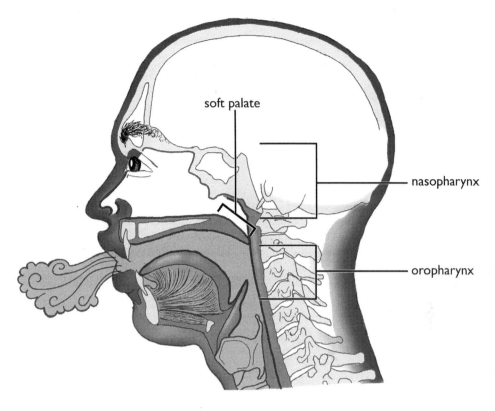

Figure 4.16 Soft palate raised. *Sandy Escobar.*

Optimizing the soft palate for singing articulation has more to do with developing greater kinesthetic awareness of its movements than stretching or strengthening the muscles that control it. Attempting to directly activate the soft palate will likely result in tensing the musculature that surrounds it rather than getting it to lift.

Here are some means of familiarizing yourself with the subtle sensations that let you know that your nasal port is closed:

- Imagine putting your head underwater (or, actually put your head underwater). Your soft palate will rise and seal off the nasal port in order to prevent water, real or imaginary, from entering your airways.

- Swallow in slow motion. You may be able to detect the ascent of the soft palate as it seals off the nasal port to prevent food from entering the nasal cavity.

- Inhale while repeatedly articulating an aspirated [k].

The soft palate reflexively ascends when it becomes necessary to seal off the nasal cavity from the rest of the pharynx. Increased awareness of this movement will help improve your ability to elicit it at will.

Articulatory Interdependence

The jaw, tongue, lips, and soft palate work together to form the sounds we make in speech. Repetition leads to the creation of habitual movement patterns, and we reinforce these patterns every time we have a conversation. The specific articulatory procedure for each phoneme we utter is stored in the brain as a neural map. For example, we typically learn to articulate [n] as a combined movement of the jaw and tongue, resulting in a neural map that says "[n] = jaw plus tongue" that we can draw on any time we need to produce this sound. The jaw, tongue, and lips, however, are capable of moving fairly independently from one another. It is possible—and, in my opinion, desirable—to articulate [n] with just a movement of the tongue and without engaging the jaw.

Optimal resonance requires that you learn to engage your articulators intentionally and with great precision to allow for as consistent a shape as possible for the resonance space—a shape that need not be *dramatically* altered each time you change vowel. Optimal definition of a given vowel is therefore the shape that takes maximum advantage of the available resonance space while generating the minimal possible disruption as you move from syllable to syllable.

Here are some guiding principles for defining vowels and consonants for singing:

Engage and move only those articulators that are essential. The jaw serves as a good example of an articulator that tends to be recruited far more often than necessary. While the jaw is typically quite active in speech, none of the vowels we articulate in singing, and very few of the consonants, require engaging the jaw. Allow the jaw to remain in a relaxed position when it is not specifically needed, and you will sing with greater ease and more consistent resonance.

Change as little as possible as you move from phoneme to phoneme. We have multiple options for articulating [i]. In habitual speech, most of us produce this sound by adjusting the position of the tongue, closing the jaw, and spreading the lips sideways. However, it is possible to articulate a resonant, intelligible [i] vowel by raising the tongue while the jaw and lips remain relaxed. Therefore, when you need to move from [ɑ] to [i], you need only move the tongue while the jaw and lips remain relaxed.

Keep articulatory action as far away from the vocal folds as possible. Given multiple possibilities for articulating a particular phoneme, choose to engage and move the articulator(s) located farther away from the vocal folds and thus least likely to encroach on their freedom. Opening the jaw beyond a certain point can compress the front of the neck in ways that may impede laryngeal freedom; if you can instead access the space you need for a given vowel by creating greater internal expansion, this is preferable to opening the jaw extremely wide. Excessive tongue activity risks entangling the hyoid bone and consequently the larynx; if you can articulate a vowel by instead engaging the lips, which have no direct attachments to the larynx, this will likely be better for overall vocal production.

While your articulators are capable of moving fairly independently from one another, practice is necessary to overcome years of muscle memory, learn to engage them separately, and coordinate their movements efficiently. In the absence of the equivalent of an articulatory ballet class, I offer the following exercises to help you begin to retrain them.

TONGUE/JAW SEPARATION

Open your jaw to the point of rotation (one or two fingers' width between your upper and lower front teeth), then press your hands against your cheeks on either side to hold this position. Using only the tip of your tongue, intone [ɑ n ɑ n ɑ n ɑ]. Repeat this exercise, substituting [t], [d], [g], and [k] for [n], encouraging your jaw to remain relaxed and uninvolved.

LIP/JAW SEPARATION

As with the former exercise, use your hands to encourage your jaw to remain in a relaxed, open position. Intone [ɑ o ɑ o ɑ o ɑ] while rounding your lips and encouraging your jaw to remain relaxed on [o].

TONGUE/LIP SEPARATION

Press your thumb gently against the underside of your jaw near your throat and again intone [ɑ o ɑ o ɑ o ɑ] while rounding your lips, encouraging the area under your thumb to remain soft and relaxed.

———————

If you find some or all of these exercises challenging, it is likely due to long-ingrained speech habits. With patience and repetition, however, you can train your articulators to move independently from one another so that articulation facilitates rather than interferes with free phonation and resonance.

When intervals or high notes that are easy for us in vocal exercises become problematic in the context of repertoire, we often assume it's a function of breath management, registration, or range. But it may actually be due to poor articulatory coordination.

If there is a phrase in your repertoire that has been confounding you, I encourage you to troubleshoot for articulation issues. Are you engaging your jaw more than necessary? Are you engaging your lips adequately on lip vowels? Does your tongue take on an appropriately arched position for each vowel, or does it retract?

Carefully choreograph the articulatory movements that take you from phoneme to phoneme in your repertoire, and you will likely enjoy freer vocal production and enhanced resonance. Even if doing so does not entirely resolve technical issues for a given phrase or interval, skillful articulation will likely simplify things to the point that you can observe other factors that may require your attention.

5

The Mind/Body Connection

Singers are simultaneously musician and instrument, inseparably integrated. When the time comes to perform, everything you have done to optimize your voice and develop your technique is set in motion by your imagination. From a strictly mechanical perspective, the breath would seem to be the generator for the vocal instrument; however, I argue that expressive intention could more accurately be said to serve this role, not merely poetically but in a literal neuromuscular sense.

The technical coordination you cultivate in the studio becomes artistically valuable only when it enables the translation of your ideas and feelings into sound. Vocalises serve to expand your range and enhance your skill at registration, but it is your ear that audiates and thereby tunes precise pitches and eliciting desired weight and dynamic levels from your vocal folds. Articulatory coordination and balanced resonance are developed through exercise and repetition, but it is through audiating each vowel and consonant that you activate the required anatomy needed to produce them. The characters you breathe life into, the narratives you weave, and the emotions you evoke must arise from creative impulse before they can be channeled through your voice.

Instrumentalists make music by manipulating an inanimate object. For them, mastery requires developing a sense of seamless integration with their instrument. The necessity of channeling their artistry through an external device rather than their own bodies would seem to set them at a disadvantage in comparison with singers, but the structural distinction between musician and instrument actually makes their job easier in some crucial ways:

Instrumentalists can visualize and feel nearly everything they are doing. They receive visual and tactile feedback from their interactions with their instrument. The muscles in the hands, arms, and mouth are relatively rich with sensory neurons; by contrast, many significant components of vocal anatomy, including the intrinsic muscles of the larynx, provide little to no sensory feedback.

They can distinguish between technique and instrument function with relative ease. Instrumentalists can simply acquire a fine model and rely on repair specialists to ensure it remains in top working condition. When a reed or a string ceases to respond properly, they can replace it, whereas you will rely on a single pair of vocal folds throughout your entire career.

The way they perceive their own sound is likely to be almost identical to the way their listeners perceive it. To a great extent, they are able to hear their own sound amplified by the acoustics of the room they're playing in rather than through the distortion of bone conduction.

The instrument they are playing is nearly identical to all others of its kind. They can emulate those with more advanced skills and compare themselves with their peers fairly objectively. This is far more difficult for singers, as each plays a unique instrument.

For singers, the difficulty of differentiating musician from instrument can make it difficult to discern whether a challenge you're experiencing stems from a technical or physiological issue. Nevertheless, I find the inherent integration of artist and instrument that singers alone enjoy to be highly advantageous, provided that we respect the relationship between mind and body and understand how we can benefit from that connection.

The Primacy of Intention

Classical singing technique can unlock the full power of the acoustic human voice, harnessing emotional extremes and vocally transmitting them to our audiences. We can set listeners' auditory apparatuses in motion, creating a sympathetic vibratory connection that exhorts them to feel what we are feeling.

However, the voice never lies—everything you are thinking and feeling will come through in your singing (see figure 5.1). If you fully immerse yourself in the experiences and emotions of the character you are embodying, you will communicate them incisively to your listeners; likewise, if you become consumed with a need to micromanage your technique or wrestle with stage fright, those activities will color your performance, because the voice is physiologically wired to respond to and communicate all your thoughts and feelings in real time.

The more vulnerable, passionate, and sincere your intentions, the more impactful your singing will be. A singer with a flawed technique can deliver a compelling performance because dramatic and musical commitment sometimes transcends imperfect coordination. Yet a singer who has little to say can deliver an impeccable performance but leave listeners cold, because virtuosity for its own sake cannot compare with raw passion.

Figure 5.1 What they think about when they sing. *Thom King.*

Mind over Matter

Hold your left arm straight out in front of you. Bend your elbow. Straighten your arm out again. How did you do that?

There are a couple of ways to answer this question. It could be said that biomechanically, you contracted your biceps, causing your elbow to flex; then you relaxed your biceps and engaged your triceps, which resulted in your arm returning to an extended position. It is equally true to say that mentally, you tasked your highly efficient neuromuscular system with executing these movements, causing a group of motor neurons to deliver your instructions to and activate the requisite musculature, with minimal conscious thought or physical effort on your part.

This mental procedure is the means whereby you are able to adjust your vocal folds to the precise length required for a given pitch, contract your diaphragm to take in the quantity of air you need to perform a phrase of a certain length, and arrange your tongue, jaw, and lips to articulate a desired vowel. Your intentions activate the neuromuscular system to initiate movement. The process may seem more mystical where the voice is concerned than for elbow movement—I find it quite magical that the vocal folds can be tuned with such specificity in response to a musical impulse!—but if you think about it, there is something magical about all human movement, as well as our ability to condition our bodies to learn new skills and improve upon old ones.

Consider the ways it is possible to augment the function of your elbow. You can improve its range of motion. You can condition it to handle greater loads by strengthening the muscles surrounding it. You can develop speed and coordination by training and repeating the movements necessary to catch and throw a baseball. But when the time comes for you to field that ball and throw it to a teammate, it is the intention to do so that reflexively sets the whole process in motion.

So it is with vocal conditioning. Flexibility, strength, and coordination are cultivated in the practice room via well-controlled movement and repetition. When the time comes to perform, you hand the controls over to your expressive intent and trust your instrument to reflexively respond.

Effective conditioning also benefits from clarity of intention. Whether you are working to balance out the musculature that supports your alignment, improve laryngeal range of motion, or coordinate your articulators, your work in both the studio and the gym is most productive when you set a well-defined agenda and commit to a procedure that will yield the results you desire. And not only the body but also the mind itself can be made more powerful through such conditioning.

Focus and Concentration

The Importance of Equanimity

Learning to sing is an open-ended endeavor. No matter how skilled and experienced you become, there will always be more to learn, refine, and express. Singing is thus both incredibly fulfilling and quite humbling. Every breakthrough reveals a higher potential level of achievement, so each success confers insight into how much more there is to learn.

Vocal progress involves exposing areas of resistance, weakness, or poor coordination so that you can work on them. Awareness is often curative, and careful observation of a problem is often enough to set in motion a process whereby you will be able to resolve that problem. However, a desire to avoid eliciting ugly or unpleasant sounds and sensations can make unmasking these problems painful. Your progress thus largely depends upon your ability to greet these revelations with equanimity.

It is essential that you remain dispassionate while observing technical flaws in your singing in order to focus your attention and energy on ameliorating them. When observing flaws provokes negative emotional reactions and self-criticism, a crucial opportunity to investigate and resolve them is lost. The most unwieldy sounds you make in the practice room often provide the very best learning opportunities—provided that rather than berate yourself you suspend judgment long enough to observe your actions and explore alternative strategies. Equanimity is therefore one of the most significant skills a singer can possess, as it lays the foundation for the swift and pleasant cultivation of all the other skills you need.

Meditation

Meditation is a means of enhancing your power of concentration. It trains the mind to observe thoughts, sensations, and other phenomena with detached awareness and expands your ability to direct your focus. While many meditation practices stem from religious traditions, meditation is now commonly taught as a stand-alone technique distinct from any dogmatic origin.

While any activity can serve as a meditative object of focus, when beginning a meditation practice it is best to set conditions that encourage a narrow focus. Try this seated meditation focusing on the body sensations associated with breathing:

1. Set a timer for a modest stretch of time, perhaps ten or fifteen minutes.

2. Sit on a chair or a cushion, assuming a posture that is comfortable but discourages slouching—a position that makes you feel alert but not rigid. Allow your hands to rest on your thighs.

3. Close your eyes and bring your awareness to your breath. Notice all movements and sensations related to breathing:

    - All movement in your abdominal area

    - The rise and fall of your ribs

    - Sensations in your throat, mouth, and nose

    - Any movement elsewhere in your body that feels related to the breath

    - Any sense of tightening or release related to the breath

    - Any changes in how expansive or shallow your breathing seems to be

    - Any sounds related to the breath

4. If your mind wanders, gently bring your awareness back to the movements and sensations related to your breath.

5. If you find yourself analyzing or judging aspects of your breathing, again gently bring your awareness back to the movements and sensations related to your breath.

This exercise exemplifies a meditation technique called Vipassana. In the West, *Vipassana* commonly translates to insight meditation, but the literal meaning of the Pali word is "to see distinctly." The version of Vipassana meditation that I practice involves observing specific phenomena and identifying, labeling, and tracking the movement of their various components. For example, as part of this exercise you could note breathing sensations of expansion and contraction or differentiate between movements, feelings, and sounds.

The mental skill facilitated by this technique is highly applicable to singing practice. Focused intention is essential when working with the mechanics of breath management in order to avoid being distracted by the sounds and sensations you elicit along the way. Heightened awareness is useful for keeping track of the individual movements of your jaw, tongue, lips, and soft palate during detailed work on articulation. Detached, dispassionate observation can enable you to gently steer your focus away from any emotional reactions you experience in relation to vocal flaws or instabilities in order to concentrate on the actions crucial for their amelioration.

Hypnotherapy

Like meditation, hypnosis promotes states of relaxed focus and awareness; in addition, it encourages greater mental suggestibility in order to reprogram specific patterns of thought and habit. While meditation provides for a general, global elevation of your ability to concentrate, hypnosis facilitates targeted psychological and behavioral shifts.

Thought patterns are habituated and stabilized in much the same way as the movement and postural patterns we cultivate, both consciously and unconsciously. Just as our movement patterns can be changed and fine-tuned, we can learn to consciously redirect our thoughts to habituate more positive and productive patterns.

For example, a history of unresolved intonation or flexibility issues may make you fear you'll never improve in these areas and cause deep discouragement. This may incline you to focus on past failures, reinforce a belief that these issues are permanent, and make it difficult to take steps to resolve them. Hypnosis offers techniques for replacing such habituated negative thought patterns with more positive, solution-oriented mental feedback loops. If you find yourself thinking, "I'll never be able to sing in tune" or "I hate how I sound right now," you can learn to redirect yourself with questions like "What would I like the sound to be? How do I want to feel when I sing this passage? What must I do to facilitate that and enjoy the process?"

Learning and skill retention are most swiftly, effectively, and pleasurably accomplished in a positive environment. When offered encouragement and rewarded with kindness, we feel motivated to absorb new information and optimistic about progress; when offered admonishment and punished with criticism, we will likely react with confusion and pain. Hypnosis can teach us to entice ourselves with carrots rather than threaten ourselves with sticks.

Somatic Disciplines

Somatic disciplines are practices that incorporate movement and mindfulness to promote mind/body integration and enhanced awareness. Humans have engaged in such disciplines for millennia—they include everything from ancient yoga and martial arts practices to modern forms of bodywork.

Somatic disciplines can improve physical coordination, kinesthetic awareness, mental focus, and emotional equanimity. They are therefore of immense benefit for singers. I will highlight several that have historically been favored by our community and discuss their potential benefits.

Yoga

Yoga is a five-thousand-year-old discipline created as a means of cultivating physical, emotional, mental, and spiritual growth and integration. Originating in India and now practiced throughout the world, yoga has evolved into numerous traditions emphasizing different aspects while sharing fundamental principles and procedures: a sequence of poses, each dynamically sustained and slowly transformed to the next, emphasizing mindfulness, acceptance, and expansive breathing.

Singers have long valued yoga for its ability to promote full breathing, balanced alignment, and calm. It encourages you to experience your body as an integrated whole and to appreciate the movement inherent in sustained stillness, which is also essential for developing a consistent musical legato.

Like singing, yoga is an open-ended practice—there are variants to suit all levels of fitness and flexibility, and there is no limit to what you can achieve. Every yoga teacher I have worked with expresses the importance of beginning where you are and letting go of outcomes and expectations—a mind-set that is also highly valuable in the voice studio.

Alexander Technique and Body Mapping

The Alexander Technique is a method of reeducating the musculoskeletal system to improve alignment and mobility, enhance performance, and alleviate chronic tension. Alexander teachers employ verbal direction and subtle touch to encourage muscular release and deepen kinesthetic awareness. They help their students become cognizant of suboptimal habitual patterns of self-use; they facilitate an experience of more efficient movement patterns and provide tools for reinforcing them.

F. Matthias Alexander was inspired to develop this technique when he found himself in need of vocal rehabilitation. When Alexander's nascent acting career was hampered by hoarseness and respiratory issues that were unresponsive to medical treatment, he theorized that his problems must somehow stem from his own behavior. Through self-examination and experimentation, he devised a means of identifying and supplanting the habits of posture and movement that had given rise to his vocal dysfunction. While the Alexander Technique is widely applicable to alleviating pain and improving performance, its origin as a means of vocal reeducation has earned it particularly high appreciation among actors and singers.

Body mapping, an offshoot of the Alexander Technique, was created by music educators to teach musicians to accurately visualize their anatomy in order to more effectively sense, train, and activate their biomechanics. Practitioners apply Alexander principles and methods to provide a guided tour of your functional anatomy, which therefore holds great value for singers seeking a practical understanding of how their instruments work.

Feldenkrais

The Feldenkrais Method employs movement and touch to expose limiting physical and psychological habits and restore healthy alignment, range of motion, and energetic flow. Like F. Matthias Alexander, Moshe Feldenkrais developed his technique out of personal necessity. When an injury left him unable to walk and existing medical protocols failed to help him recover, he drew on his background in physics, engineering, and martial arts to devise a means to restore his own mobility. Feldenkrais is taught in both one-on-one "Functional Integration" sessions with a certified practitioner and in group "Awareness through Movement" classes.

Singers value Feldenkrais for its application of targeted kinesthetic suggestion to retrain alignment and expand breathing. A key principle of Feldenkrais is the idea of "passive control"— initiating movement by formulating a clear intention rather than physical effort. It is therefore useful for helping singers learn to allow expressive intent to engage the singing voice, rather than muscular manipulation.

The Practice of Singing

In addition to practices profiled in this chapter, there exist a wealth of mental disciplines and somatic methods that can complement and heighten your work in the studio. Explore the options available in your area, and keep in mind that finding a skilled, experienced practitioner is often of greater importance than the particular modality they espouse.

One of the things I most love about singing is that it is itself a practice that serves to integrate body and mind. Meditation, yoga, and martial arts can improve mental and physical well-being in countless ways, but these practices are most rewarding when pursued as ends unto themselves rather than as means to particular goals. Learn to approach your singing practice as its own end, and you may find that the resulting enhancement of focus, self-awareness, and expressive power serves to enrich all your activities, musical and otherwise.

6

A Singer-Centered Workout Regimen

Exercise scientists have become adept at tailoring sport-specific training regimens for different types of athletes. A great deal is known about how to optimize the body for endurance, power, speed, balance, and so on. While there are notable exceptions, elite athletes in a given sport usually share a common body type and follow a similar sport-specific training protocol.

By contrast, the variety of body types we see on the operatic stage is breathtaking in its diversity. While the basic anatomy and skill set required for singing may be common to all and many of the singers in a given Fach share some physical similarities, many of the things that make a singer exceptional stem from unique anatomical attributes rather than conformity to a physical ideal. Therefore, while there are certainly fitness strategies that all singers are likely to find useful, the training regimen best suited to optimize an individual singer's body for peak performance will be unique to that singer.

Just as achieving a foundational level of vocal technique is a prerequisite for the performance of classical literature, establishing a fundamental level of awareness, stabilization, and skill is essential for engaging in a fitness program. The exercises presented in this chapter have been chosen to address common postural distortions, establish a balance of strength and flexibility, and promote good exercise form. These movements provide a comprehensive workout in themselves, while also preparing you to eventually undertake a more rigorous strength-training regimen, engage in dance or stage combat training, or excel at the recreational sport of your choice.

Reference the data you gathered from the assessments in chapter 1 in order to craft the fitness regimen best suited to your particular needs, strengths, and challenges. Feel free to explore all of the exercises I have included here while focusing on those designed to promote flexibility in the muscles you identified as tight and strengthen those that are relatively weak.

Here are some general guidelines to keep in mind throughout your workout:

Breathe. Any number of things may incline you to hold your breath while exercising, including the demands of concentration and an instinct to valve off the glottis to stabilize the torso. Continuous, full breathing is essential for good form as well as for ensuring adequate oxygen supply. When performing strength-training movements, it is generally advisable to exhale while lifting weights (or your own body, as the case may be) and to inhale while lowering.

Keep your face and neck relaxed. Maintain a loose, flabby feeling in your throat and avoid clenching your jaw. Never engage in the Valsalva maneuver—the tight glottal closure that results in the grunting you frequently hear from bodybuilders. Keep your chin gently tucked down toward your chest and frequently remind yourself to release the back of your neck and your upper trapezius.

Focus on the functional goal of each exercise. The point of a strength-training exercise is conditioning a specific muscle, not seeing how heavy a dumbbell you can lift; the point of a flexibility exercise is improving the range of motion of a given joint rather than seeing how far you can pull yourself in one direction or another.

Prioritize movements and modalities that emphasize balance and stability. Exercises that require you to stabilize your core and joints and challenge your balance will enhance your ability to execute stage movement while continuing to manage your breath well.

Listen to your body. Any effective exercise regimen is characterized by a degree of effort and discomfort, so it's important to evaluate whether the effort and discomfort are facilitating or interfering with your progress. While some muscle fatigue and discomfort are to be expected, joint pain indicates a need to adjust your form or discontinue the exercise. When performing a new exercise or engaging a muscle group for the first time in a while, err on the side of doing too little in order to avoid excessive soreness and to speed your recovery time.

Modify movements as necessary. If you find a particular exercise prohibitively difficult or uncomfortable, seek an alternative movement targeting the same muscle groups. I have offered modifications for many of the strength-training exercises to make them simpler and more accessible.

Self-Myofascial Release

Self-myofascial release (SMR) provides a deep tissue massage for tight muscles, enhancing the impact of subsequent flexibility and strength-training exercises. SMR warms up the web of connective tissue that surrounds muscle tissue and softens adhesions causing chronic tension. When the connective tissue surrounding a muscle group is warmer and more pliable during exercise, growth and adaptations in that muscle group are often achieved more swiftly and effectively.

To perform SMR with a foam roller, position the targeted muscle on the roller so as to place as much of your body weight as possible on top of it while supporting yourself with your arms and/ or legs. Slowly roll along the full length of the muscle. Pause at any point that feels particularly tender, continuing to breathe while sustaining the position for thirty seconds.

SMR for the Shoulders: Middle and Lower Trapezius, Rhomboids, and Intercostals

Sit on a mat with the foam roller behind your hips. Bring your knees up and place your feet flat on the floor. Lie back on the foam roller, positioning your lower ribs on top of it. Using your hands to support your head and neck, lean back and raise your hips off the floor so that most of your weight is on the roller, as shown in figure 6.1. Slowly walk your feet forward so that the roller moves from your lower ribs up toward your neck, allowing your head and shoulders to descend toward the floor. Continue until you feel the roller at the top of your shoulders, then reverse direction until the roller is once again at your lower ribs. If you find a point of particular tenderness or tightness along your back or shoulders, pause in that position and continue breathing until the sensation subsides.

Figure 6.1 Self–myofascial release for the shoulders. *Daniel Welch.*

SMR for the Latissimus Dorsi

Lie on a mat on one side with the arm closest to the mat extended in front of you. Place the foam roller under your uppermost ribs close to your armpit. Place the foot of the upper leg on the mat in front of the knee of the lower leg. Use the upper leg to lift the lower hip off the floor so that most of your weight is now resting on the foam roller, as shown in figure 6.2. Push off with your foot and roll your body so that the foam roller moves down your side, then change direction so that it returns to the starting position near your armpit. If you find a point of particular tenderness or tightness along your side or back, pause in that position and continue breathing until the sensation subsides. Repeat on the other side.

Figure 6.2 Self-myofascial release for the latissimus dorsi. *Daniel Welch.*

SMR for the Hamstrings

Sit on a mat with your legs extended in front of you and the foam roller under your knees. Place your hands on the mat on either side of your hips, then lift your hips up so that most of your weight is on the roller. Cross one leg over the other, as shown in figure 6.3. Roll yourself forward so that the roller moves up the back of your leg to your hip, then roll in the other direction so that it returns to your knee. If you find a point of particular tenderness or tightness along your leg, pause in that position and continue breathing until the sensation subsides. Repeat on the other side.

Figure 6.3 Self-myofascial release for the hamstrings. *Daniel Welch.*

SMR for the Quadriceps and Hip Flexors

This version of SMR employs a massage stick rather than a foam roller (see figure 6.4). In a seated position, cross one leg over the other. Beginning at the hip, apply a massage stick with firm pressure to the front of the upper leg. Slowly roll it toward the knee, then back up to the hip. Repeat several times. If you find a point of particular tenderness or tightness along your leg, roll the stick repeatedly over the point of tension until it feels smoother and less tender. Repeat on the other side.

Figure 6.4 Self-myofascial release for the quadriceps and hip flexors. *Daniel Welch.*

SMR for the Calves

Sit on a mat with your legs extended in front of you and place the foam roller under your ankles (see figure 6.5). Place your hands on the mat on either side of your hips, then lift your hips up so most of your weight is on the roller. Cross one leg over the other. Roll yourself forward so the roller moves up the back of your calf to your knee, then roll in the other direction so that the roller returns to your ankle, repeating this movement several times. If you find a point of particular tenderness or tightness along the calf, pause in that position and continue breathing until the sensation subsides. Repeat on the other side.

Figure 6.5 Self-myofascial release for the calves. *Daniel Welch.*

Massage for the Upper Trapezius

The upper trapezius elevates the shoulders, so tightness in this muscle can lead to neck tension. It is therefore particularly important for singers to relax this area. The upper trapezius is difficult to target with a foam roller or massage stick, so I recommend using massage, either with your hand or an electric massager. Focus on the area just to the side of your neck, squeezing it with the thumb and fingers of the opposite arm or holding a massager firmly to the spot (see figure 6.6). Allow your arm to dangle by your side with the elbow extended, then slowly elevate the shoulder, roll it around to the back, and then lower it to the starting position. Repeat this cyclical movement several times, taking care not to rotate the shoulder forward. Repeat on the other side.

Figure 6.6 Massage for the upper trapezius. *Daniel Welch.*

Static Stretching

Static stretching improves flexibility in muscles and connective tissue, increasing joint range of motion. It involves holding positions that encourage targeted muscles to lengthen and gradually help them extend further. In order to perform a static stretch effectively, you must hold it for a minimum of thirty seconds. Stretches should be performed in a sustained fashion rather than by bouncing in and out of position.

Static Stretch for the Latissimus Dorsi

Kneel in front of a stability ball. Place both hands on top of the ball and slowly roll it away from you, folding forward at the hip and inclining your head and torso toward the floor so that your arms stretch up and back, as shown in figure 6.7. Continue breathing and hold the stretch for a minimum of thirty seconds. Release the stretch by rolling the ball back toward you and sitting back on your heels.

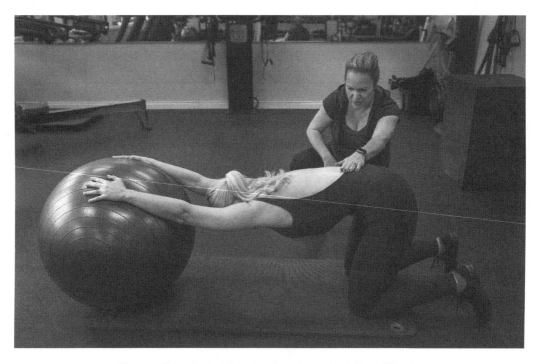

Figure 6.7 Static stretch for the latissimus dorsi. *Daniel Welch.*

Static Stretch for the Pectoralis Major and Minor

Stand facing an open door frame or a stable pillar. With your upper arm parallel to the floor and your elbow flexed to a 90-degree angle, place a forearm vertically against the door frame or pillar so that it makes firm contact from your palm all the way to the elbow, as shown in figure 6.8. Lean forward until you feel a stretch in your upper chest. Hold the stretch for a minimum of thirty seconds, then repeat the stretch on the other side.

Figure 6.8 Static stretch for the pectoralis major and minor. *Daniel Welch.*

Half-Angel Stretch for the Shoulders

The half-angel stretch is a dynamic stretch. Unlike static stretches, which sustain a single position targeting release of a single muscle group, dynamic stretches employ movements that encourage multiple muscle groups to release in order to promote balance between them. Our shoulder blades, or scapulae, provide attachment points for most of the important muscles of the shoulders, back, and chest, so this dynamic stretch is useful for warming up and lengthening them all.

Lie on your back on a mat with your arms extended over your head. Bring your knees up and place your feet flat on the floor, as shown in figure 6.9. Slowly bend your elbows and draw your arms down toward your sides until your elbows are level with your shoulders as shown in figure 6.10, keeping both wrists and elbows on the mat or as close to it as possible throughout. Reverse the movement, slowly extending your arms over your head and returning to the starting position, again keeping wrists and elbows on or near the mat. Repeat the movement four to six times.

Figure 6.9 Half-angel shoulder stretch, starting position. *Daniel Welch.*

Figure 6.10 Half-angel shoulder stretch, movement. *Daniel Welch.*

Static Stretch for the Hamstrings

Sit on a mat with your right leg extended in front of you with your knee and toes pointing straight up. Place your left foot against your right inner thigh, keeping the left knee on the floor if possible. Sit tall with your spine in good alignment. Fold forward from the hip over the right leg while maintaining a well-aligned spine. Reach for your right calf or ankle with your left hand, as shown in figure 6.11, and gently pull your chest closer to your leg without compromising your alignment. Hold the stretch for a minimum of thirty seconds. You may find that you do not have to fold very far forward at all in order to feel a stretch, so remember that the point is not to move your chest closer to your knee but rather to stretch your hamstrings. Repeat with the left leg.

Figure 6.11 Static stretch for the hamstrings. *Daniel Welch.*

Static Stretch for the Hip Adductors

Sit on a mat with your right leg extended to the side at a comfortable angle, with your knee and toes pointing straight up. Place your left foot against your upper right thigh. Sit tall with your spine in good alignment. Extend your arms in front of you and fold forward from the hip while maintaining a well-aligned spine, as shown in figure 6.12. Rest your fingertips on the floor. Hold the stretch for a minimum of thirty seconds. You may find that you do not have to fold very far forward at all in order to feel a stretch, so remember that the point is not to move your chest closer to your knee but rather to stretch your hip adductors. Repeat with the left leg.

Figure 6.12 Static stretch for the hip adductors. *Daniel Welch.*

Static Stretch for the Quadriceps and Hip Flexors

Stand near a wall or column and place your left hand against it for balance. Stand on your left leg, flex your right knee, and grasp your right foot behind you with your right hand. Align your right knee with the left and draw your knees together. To stretch your quadriceps, gently pull your right foot closer to your buttocks, as shown in figure 6.13. Hold the stretch for a minimum of thirty seconds. To stretch your hip flexors, pull the right leg farther back and up, as shown in figure 6.14. Hold the stretch for a minimum of thirty seconds. Repeat for the left leg.

Figure 6.13 Static stretch for the quadriceps. *Daniel Welch.*

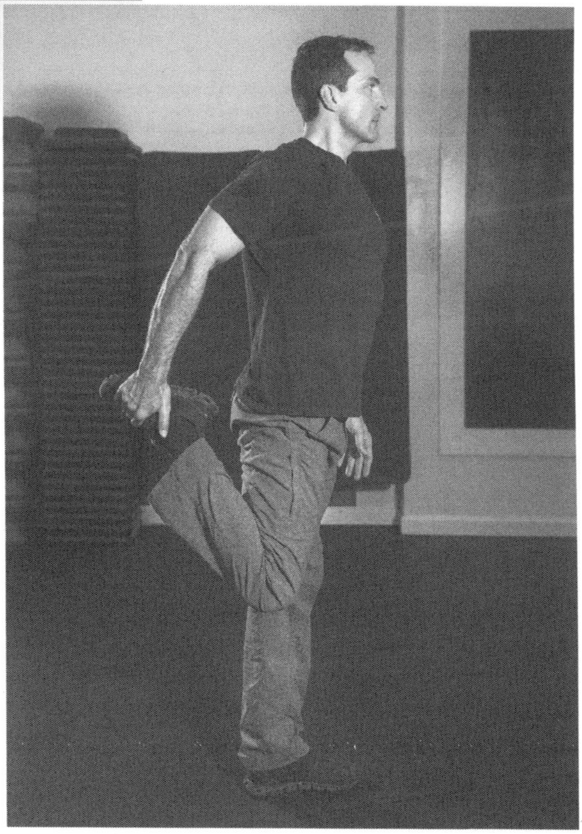

Figure 6.14 Static stretch for the hip flexors. *Daniel Welch.*

Static Stretch for the Calves: Gastrocnemius and Soleus

Two muscles comprise the calf; each requires a slightly different position for an effective static stretch. To stretch the gastrocnemius, extend one leg back, keeping the knee straight, the back heel on the floor and the toe of the back foot pointing straight forward rather than out to the side. Keeping your torso upright and in good alignment, place your hands on the knee of the front leg for support. Bend the knee of the front leg until you feel a stretch in the calf of the rear leg, as shown in figure 6.15. Hold the stretch for a minimum of thirty seconds. To stretch the soleus, maintain the same position but bend the back knee slightly, being sure to keep the back heel on the floor, as shown in figure 6.16. You should feel the point of stretch shift a little lower and more to the inside of the calf. Hold this stretch for a minimum of thirty seconds. Repeat both stretches for the other leg.

Figure 6.15 Static stretch for the gastrocnemius. *Daniel Welch.*

Figure 6.16 Static stretch for the soleus. *Daniel Welch.*

Static Stretch for the Rib Cage: The Intercostal Muscles

Static stretches for your rib cage can help remind you to breathe fully throughout the rest of your workout. Include them in your vocal warm-up as well to promote full range of motion for your rib cage while singing.

To stretch the front of the rib cage, sit on a stability ball and walk yourself forward until your torso drapes backward over the ball, as shown in figure 6.17. Take a moment to get your balance; then take a few deep, slow breaths, expanding your ribs all the way up to your collarbone. Then take another full breath, continuing to try to inhale beyond the point you can take in any more air, effectively holding your breath with the continuous engagement of your muscles of inspiration. Sustain for three seconds, then exhale. Repeat three or four times. Return to your starting position by walking your feet back so that you are sitting on the ball.

Figure 6.17 Static stretch for the rib cage, front. *Daniel Welch.*

To stretch the back of the rib cage, kneel in front of the stability ball. Place your chest on top of the ball and roll forward so that your torso is draped over the ball, with your fingertips and toes on the floor, as shown in figure 6.18. Take a few deep, slow breaths, expanding your ribs as far as possible in the back. Then take another full breath, continuing to try to inhale beyond the point you can take in any more air, effectively holding your breath with the continuous engagement of your muscles of inspiration. Sustain for three seconds, then exhale. Repeat three or four times. Return to your starting position by rolling back until you return to a kneeling position.

Figure 6.18 Static stretch for the rib cage, back. *Daniel Welch.*

Strength and Stabilization Training

Strength training improves muscle function by working muscles to the point of fatigue. These exercises paradoxically injure muscle cells to their benefit, instigating a recovery cycle that not only repairs but also stimulates growth in the muscle cells. While the process results in stronger, more clearly defined muscles, engaging in a balanced strength training regimen is unlikely to add significant bulk to your profile unless you pursue this as a goal.

Most of the exercises presented in this chapter include a stabilization component, offering a neuromuscular challenge as well as a strength challenge. Exercises that require you to maintain your balance or perform asymmetrical movements help develop optimal length/tension relationships between muscle groups.

When possible and applicable, I have appended modified versions to each exercise to make them simpler, more challenging, more aesthetically impactful, and/or easier to perform in a hotel room with minimal equipment.

The strategy I have applied throughout this section to accentuate muscle groups considered to have aesthetic appeal involves alternating sets of exercises that promote stability and improved alignment with sets of exercises that target the same muscles but provide for an overload increase. Muscles become stronger in response to overload—the requirement to meeting challenges that are greater than what they are regularly subjected to. If you wish to develop visibly larger, well-defined muscles, it is therefore necessary to increase the demand being placed upon them. You can safely incorporate aesthetic goals into your regimen, provided that you do so in moderation and work to build strength throughout your instrument rather than focusing exclusively on the glamor muscles.

Lat Pulldown

Performing lat pulldowns with good form not only helps to resolve common upper-body posture imbalances but also establishes the shoulder stability singers need for breath management. This exercise targets the latissimus dorsi, rhomboids, middle and lower trapezius, and biceps.

Sit on a stability ball facing a cable machine with arms positioned at ten o'clock and two o'clock and set the weight at a moderately challenging level to ensure good form. Set up your starting position with care, as shown in figures 6.19 and 6.20. Grasp the handles and sit tall with elbows fully extended, being sure to draw your shoulder blades together and down, as shown in figure 6.21. Draw your elbows in toward your sides with palms continuing to face forward, as far as you can without rotating your shoulders forward, as shown in figures 6.22 and 6.23. As you extend your elbows to return to the starting position, continue to keep your shoulder blades retracted so that your shoulders do not elevate as shown in figure 6.24. Perform this movement slowly, about four seconds in each direction, with smooth transitions between lifting and lowering. Exhale as you pull the cables down and inhale as you return to the starting position. Aim for two to three sets of twelve to fifteen repetitions.

Figure 6.19 Lat pulldown, starting position, back view. *Daniel Welch.*

Figure 6.20 Lat pulldown, starting position, side view. *Daniel Welch.*

Figure 6.21 Shoulder blade retraction. *Daniel Welch.*

Figure 6.22 Lat pulldown, movement, back view. *Daniel Welch.*

Figure 6.23 Lat pulldown, movement, side view. *Daniel Welch.*

Figure 6.24 Shoulder elevation. *Daniel Welch.*

Stabilization challenge. Complete the initial pulldown with both arms, as shown in figures 6.22 and 6.23. Sustain the pulldown position with your left arm and return only your right arm to the starting position, keeping your core and both shoulders stable and keeping your weight centered on the stability ball. Pull down with the right arm, hold it in place, and return your left arm to the starting position. Continue to alternate your arms throughout the set.

Lat pulldowns on the go. Lat pulldowns can be performed using a resistance band with handles and a door anchor (see "Additional Resources"). Anchor the resistance band to the top of a door. Position a chair facing the door, far enough away from the door so that when you are seated and grasp the handles of the resistance band with your arms extended there is already a bit of tension in the band. Sit tall on the chair with good alignment and your feet flat on the floor. Grasp the handles with your elbows fully extended and tilt forward from your hips. Maintain a stable neutral spine and perform the lat pulldowns from this position. Your hands and forearms will be closer together for your starting position than when doing this movement with a cable machine, but their position at the bottom of the movement should be the same as shown in figures 6.22 and 6.23.

Cable Chest Press

This exercise targets the pectoralis major, pectoralis minor, and triceps. Assume a split stance with your back to a cable machine with arms positioned at nine o'clock and three o'clock. Your hips, knees, and ankles should align vertically on both sides with knees slightly flexed and both feet pointing straight forward. Your torso should remain upright—take care not to lean forward as you perform the movement. Set the weight at only a moderately challenging level to ensure good form. Grasp the handles and set up your starting position with care. Your upper arms should be parallel to the floor and your elbows flexed at a right angle so that your wrists are aligned with your elbows, as shown in figures 6.25 and 6.26. As with the lat pulldown, keep your shoulder blades retracted throughout the movement. Extend your arms forward and bring your hands together in front of your sternum, as shown in figures 6.27 and 6.28. Return to the starting position. Your shoulders and elbows should move in tandem—avoid straightening your arms first and pulling your hands together second. Perform this movement slowly, about four seconds in each direction, with smooth transitions between lifting and lowering. Exhale as you press the cables forward and inhale as you return to the starting position. Aim for two to three sets of twelve to fifteen repetitions.

Simplified cable chest press. Perform this exercise in a seated position. Place a workout bench set in an upright position in front of the cable machine with its back to the machine. Your torso should remain upright with your shoulders resting against the bench throughout the movement—do not lean forward. Grasp the handles with your upper arms parallel to the floor and your elbows flexed at a right angle; perform the movement as described above.

Stabilization challenge. Sustain the starting position with your left arm and press forward and extend only your right arm so that your right hand is directly in front of your sternum, keeping your core and both shoulders stable and keeping your weight centered between your legs. Return your right arm to the starting position, and perform the movement with your left arm. Continue to alternate your arms throughout the set.

Figure 6.25 Cable chest press, starting position, front view. *Daniel Welch.*

Figure 6.26 Cable chest press, starting position, side view. *Daniel Welch.*

Figure 6.27 Cable chest press, movement, front view. *Daniel Welch.*

Figure 6.28 Cable chest press, movement, side view. *Daniel Welch.*

Glamor factor—pecs. Alternate sets of this exercise with either barbell bench presses or seated machine chest presses. When performing any variety of chest press, position your hands at shoulder's width apart; when your arms are extended at the top of the lift, they should be in front of your sternum, not in front of your face. Do not increase the weight beyond your ability to keep your shoulders stable throughout the movement, as anything that encourages your shoulders to elevate or rotate internally will be counterproductive for your singing.

Cable chest press on the go. Chest presses can be performed using a resistance band with handles and a door anchor. Anchor the resistance band to a door. Position a chair facing away from the door, far enough away from the door so that when you are seated and grasp the handles of the resistance band in the chest press starting position there is already a bit of tension in the band. Sit tall on the chair with good alignment and your feet flat on the floor. Grasp the handles with your upper arms parallel to the floor and your elbows flexed at a right angle so that your wrists are aligned with your elbows, as shown in figures 6.25 and 6.26. Extend your arms forward and bring your hands together in front of your sternum; then return to the starting position.

Single Leg Scaption

This exercise promotes stability of the core and lumbo-pelvic-hip complex and targets the rhomboids and middle and lower trapezius.

Stand tall with good alignment, with feet about hip width apart, toes pointing straight forward and arms resting at your sides. Retract your shoulder blades and slowly raise one leg, bending your knee, until the knee is level with the hip, as shown in figure 6.29. Take as much time as necessary to get your balance and avoid collapsing into the hip or locking the knee of the standing leg. Raise your arms up at a 45-degree angle until your hands are level with your head, as shown in figure 6.30, keeping your balance and continuing to retract your shoulder blades. Then lower your arms to the starting position while continuing to balance on one leg. Keep the knee and foot of the lifted leg pointing straight forward rather than allowing your hip to turn out. Perform this movement slowly, about four seconds in each direction, with smooth transitions between lifting and lowering. Exhale as you lift your arms and inhale as you lower them. Aim for two to three sets of twelve to fifteen repetitions. This movement can be performed with or without dumbbells. When using dumbbells, light weights are enough to make this exercise sufficiently challenging.

Simplified scaption. Perform the arm movement with both feet on the floor.

Glamor factor—delts. Alternate sets of this exercise with sets of dumbbell lateral raises. Stand tall with good alignment, with feet about hip width apart, toes pointing straight forward and arms resting at your sides and a dumbbell of moderate weight in each hand. Keeping your shoulder blades retracted and elbows extended, turn your palms to face forward and slowly raise both arms up so they are level with your shoulders. Lower your arms to the starting position and repeat. Exhale as you lift your arms and inhale as you lower them.

Single leg scaption on the go. You can perform this exercise using a light resistance band with handles. Grasp both handles of the resistance band and step on it with the leg you intend to balance on. You may need to loop and shorten it in order to set up a starting position with tension in the band. Perform the movement of the exercise as described above. This modification also provides an increased stabilization challenge.

Figure 6.29 Single leg scaption, starting position. *Daniel Welch.*

Figure 6.30 Single leg scaption, movement. *Daniel Welch.*

Dumbbell Split Squat

This exercise promotes stability of the lumbo-pelvic-hip complex and targets all major muscles of the legs.

Assume a split stance with the knee of the front leg flexed, the back leg straight, and your arms extended by your sides, as shown in figure 6.31. Your hips, knees, and ankles should align vertically on both sides with feet pointing straight forward—avoid allowing the toe of the back leg to point out to the side. Your torso should remain upright with your shoulders aligned over your hips—take care not to lean forward as you perform the movement or allow your lower back to arch. Lower toward the floor by increasing the angle at which the front knee is bent, but do not descend far enough to allow the back knee to touch the floor, as shown in figure 6.32; then return to the starting position. Try to keep your hips square throughout the movement rather than allowing the hip of the front leg to elevate. Perform this movement slowly, about four seconds in each direction, with smooth transitions between moving down and up. Inhale as you squat and exhale as you raise yourself up. Aim for two to four sets of twelve to fifteen repetitions, alternating front and back legs between each set. This movement can be performed with or without dumbbells. Adding dumbbells increases the intensity of the exercise while making it easier to balance in this asymmetrical position.

Simplified split squat. Substitute a curtsy squat. This is a movement that may prove directly applicable in performance. Stand tall with good alignment, with feet about hip width apart, toes pointing straight forward and arms resting at your sides. Keeping your torso upright with both hips and shoulders facing forward, step back with your left leg and place your left toe behind and to the right of your right leg; bend both knees and squat toward the floor. Push off with your left foot to return to the starting position. Repeat, alternating sides.

Glamor factor—glutes. Alternate sets of this exercise with sets of leg presses. Leg press machines enable a squat movement from a seated position and provide a measure of stability in order to perform the movement with increased load. Sit on the seat and adjust the footplate so that your ankles, knees, and hips are aligned with one another at 90-degree angles. Extend your legs to push the footplate away, then smoothly reverse the movement and return to the starting position. Exhale as you press and inhale on the return.

Single Leg Squat Touchdown

This exercise promotes stability of the lumbo-pelvic-hip complex and core and targets all major muscles of the legs.

Stand tall with good alignment, with feet about hip width apart, toes pointing straight forward and arms resting at your sides. Place your left hand on your hip and raise your right leg an inch or two above the ground, by bending your right knee; allow the right foot to dangle close to the left foot without actually touching it, as shown in figure 6.33. Take as much time as necessary to get your balance, avoiding collapsing into the hip or locking the knee of the standing leg. Maintaining good upper-body alignment, squat down by folding from your hips and bending the left knee, reaching your right hand toward the left ankle, as shown in figure 6.34. Keep the right and left ankles aligned rather than allowing the right foot to move back. Try to keep your hips square throughout the movement rather than allowing the hip of the left leg to elevate. Slowly come all the way back

Figure 6.31 Dumbbell split squat, starting position. *Daniel Welch.*

Figure 6.32 Dumbbell split squat, movement. *Daniel Welch.*

up to the starting position, taking a moment to stabilize your balance before beginning the next repetition. Perform this movement slowly, about four seconds in each direction, with smooth transitions between moving down and up. Inhale as you squat and exhale as you raise yourself up. Aim for two to four sets of twelve to fifteen repetitions, alternating left and right legs between each set. This movement can be performed with or without a dumbbell in the hand of the reaching arm. Adding a dumbbell increases the intensity of the exercise while making it easier to balance in this asymmetrical position.

Figure 6.33 Single leg squat touchdown, starting position. *Daniel Welch.*

Simplified single leg squat. Return to standing on both feet in between repetitions, then once again slowly and carefully get your balance on one leg before continuing.

Integration challenge. Perform the squat while holding a dumbbell. As you ascend, bend the elbow of the arm holding the dumbbell into a biceps curl; when you are fully upright, extend the arm straight up over your shoulder into an overhead press. Bring the arm back down into a biceps curl, and then reach with it toward the standing leg as you move into the next squat.

Figure 6.34 Single leg squat touchdown, movement. *Daniel Welch.*

Glamor factor—calves. Alternate this exercise with sets of calf raises. Stand tall with good alignment, with feet about hip width apart, toes pointing straight forward and arms resting at your sides. Slowly lift your heels off the floor so that you are balancing on both toes. Sustain this position for two to four seconds, lower your heels toward the floor, and then without returning your weight to your heels, reverse the movement and balance on your toes again.

Multi-Planar Balance/Reach

This exercise promotes stability of the core and lumbo-pelvic-hip complex. Stand tall with good alignment, with feet about hip width apart, toes pointing straight forward and hands on your hips. Slowly raise one leg, bending your knee, until the knee is level with the hip. Maintain your balance and extend the leg straight in front of you, as shown in figure 6.35, and then return to the starting position with the knee bent in front of the hip. Repeat the movement, extending the leg at a 45-degree angle as shown in figure 6.36, then return to the starting position with the knee bent in front of the hip. Repeat the movement, extending the leg to the side as shown in figure 6.37, then return to the starting position. Avoid locking the knee of the standing leg. Repeat the movement while balancing on the other leg. Perform the full cycle three to six times for each side.

A Balanced Core Workout

The concern about exercise I most frequently hear from singers is whether, and how intensely, they ought to work out their abdominal muscles. A strong, balanced core musculature provides exceptional support for your singing technique. My advice is therefore to develop as much strength and flexibility throughout your core muscles as you can, making sure to take a comprehensive and balanced approach. Residual tightness in your abdominal muscles only results when you emphasize some muscle groups while neglecting others and/or fail to stretch properly. Here is a core workout designed with balance in mind.

Plank

This exercise promotes core stabilization. Kneel on a mat and then move into a tabletop position with your forearms on the mat in front of you. Align your hips with your knees and your shoulders with your elbows. Establish good alignment of your spine in this position, being sure to avoid pulling your head up, humping up your shoulders, or either arching or straightening out your lower back. Draw your navel in toward your spine to stabilize it, then step your feet back so that your legs are straight with your toes on the floor. Slowly lower your hips so that your back and legs form a straight line, as shown in figure 6.38. Continue to breathe while holding this position for as long as you can without compromising form. Then return to the starting tabletop position, on your elbows and knees. Repeat three to five times. Aim to hold the position fifteen to thirty seconds.

The plank can be tricky to master because it's difficult to see and feel what you're doing. Try to position yourself by a mirror where you can turn your head a bit to the side to evaluate your alignment. One common compensation is humping the shoulders up, as shown in figure 6.39. If you find yourself doing this, try to drop your shoulders down while keeping your hips from also dropping. Another compensation is to arch the lower back, as shown in figure 6.40. If you observe this, tilt your pelvis forward until the curve of your lower back is no longer exaggerated.

Figure 6.35 Multiplanar balance/reach, extension to the front. *Daniel Welch.*

Figure 6.36 Multiplanar balance/reach, extension to a 45-degree angle. *Daniel Welch.*

Figure 6.37 Multiplanar balance/reach, extension to the side. *Daniel Welch.*

Figure 6.38 Plank. *Daniel Welch.*

Figure 6.39 Plank with shoulder compensation. *Daniel Welch.*

Figure 6.40 Plank with arched lower back compensation. *Daniel Welch.*

Simplified plank. Begin on your hands and knees with your arms extended and your hands aligned underneath your shoulders, rather than down on your elbows and fists.

Stabilization challenge. Establish your plank position with good form, then slowly lift one leg off the floor so that all your weight is on the other foot. Continue to breathe while holding this position for ten seconds, then slowly switch legs and repeat.

Superman

This exercise targets the spinal extensors, gluteus maximus, gluteus minimus, and hamstrings.

Lie facedown on a mat with your arms extended slightly out to the side near your hips, palms down, as shown in figure 6.41. Engage the muscles in your lower back and butt to simultaneously raise your upper body and legs as high off the mat as you can, as shown in figure 6.42. Tuck your chin down toward your chest. Continue to breathe while holding this position for as long as you can without compromising form. Then lower your body and legs to the mat and rest for a moment. Repeat three to five times. Aim to hold the position fifteen to twenty seconds.

Strength challenge. Rather than beginning with your arms by your sides, extend your arms over your head with your palms facing down. This is the position from which the exercise takes its name, and it increases the load placed on the muscles of the lower back. Raise your arms in this overhead position as you perform the movement, continuing to reach up and forward as though flying like Superman.

Figure 6.41 Superman starting position. *Daniel Welch.*

Figure 6.42 Superman movement. *Daniel Welch.*

Trunk Rotation

This exercise targets the transversus abdominis, internal and external obliques, and deep core stabilizers.

Facing a cable machine at the cable's point of origin, assume a split stance with your right leg forward and your left leg behind. Adjust the cable so that the point where it emerges from the machine is level with your sternum. Grasp the handle with both hands with arms extended, as shown in figure 6.43. Your hips, knees, and ankles should align vertically on both sides with knees

Figure 6.43 Trunk rotation starting position. *Daniel Welch.*

slightly flexed and both feet pointing straight forward. Maintaining good upper-body alignment, keeping your arms extended and your hips square, pivot to the left using only your abdominal and core muscles as shown in figure 6.44, then return to the starting position. It should feel as though the cable is attached to your midsection rather than your arms. Perform this movement slowly, about four seconds in each direction, with smooth transitions between rotating to the left and returning to the right. Exhale as you pivot left and inhale as you return to the right. Aim for two to four sets of twelve to fifteen repetitions, alternating sides between each set.

Figure 6.44 Trunk rotation movement. *Daniel Welch.*

Simplified trunk rotation. Perform the movement from a seated position. Sit on a workout bench facing the cable machine at the cable's point of origin. Adjust the cable so that the point where it emerges from the machine is level with your sternum, and grasp the handle with both hands with arms extended. Keep your feet flat on the floor with your knees aligned with your ankles. With arms extended and your hips square, pivot to the left using only your abdominal and core muscles, and then return to the starting position. Decrease the weight if you find that your knees counter the movement by pivoting to the right. Alternate sides between sets.

Trunk rotation on the go. Trunk rotations can be performed using a resistance band with handles and a door anchor. Anchor the resistance band to a door in a position that is level with your sternum. Step back until you feel the desired level of resistance in the band and perform the exercise as described above.

Ball Crunch

A strong rectus abdominis, aka "six-pack," supports the lower back and contributes to breath management. However, crunches are much maligned by singers because when performed improperly or in the absence of other abdominal exercises, they can do more harm than good. Remember that the point of this movement is to bring your rib cage closer to your pelvis by flexing the lower back, not to sit up. My recommended arm position, with fingertips behind the ears and elbows out to the sides, will help you avoid the temptation to pull on your neck. Performing the movement on the stability ball keeps the muscles of the core engaged, promoting more balanced abdominal development. Keep your chin tucked gently to your chest throughout the movement.

This exercise targets the rectus abdominis and stabilizes the lumbo-pelvic-hip complex.

Sit on a stability ball and then walk your body forward while leaning back until your hips and lower back are on top of the ball. Keeping your core and leg muscles engaged to stabilize your position on the ball, lie back on the ball and place your fingertips behind your ears, pointing your elbows straight out to either side, as shown in figure 6.45. Begin to draw your lower ribs closer to your pelvis by slowly curling up the vertebrae of your lower back, as shown in figure 6.46. Continue until you are sitting nearly all the way up, as shown in figure 6.47, and then reverse the movement by gradually uncurling your vertebrae until you have returned to the starting position. Keep your elbows pointing straight out to the sides throughout the movement and your chin tucked slightly toward your chest. Do not pull on your neck. Perform this movement slowly with smooth transitions between curling up and uncurling down. Exhale as you come up and inhale as you lower. Aim for two to three sets of twelve to fifteen repetitions. When you are finished, lie back over the ball and breathe deeply for a few moments as described in the rib cage stretch to give your abs a stretch.

Simplified crunch. Perform only the descending portion of the crunch movement, on a mat rather than on a stability ball. Sit with your feet on the floor and knees up. Place your fingertips behind your ears and point your elbows straight out to the side. Round your back forward. As slowly as possible, tilt back from your hips and gradually uncurl your spine, placing it on the mat one vertebra at a time until you are lying on the mat. After a brief rest, use your hands to push yourself back up into the starting position and repeat the movement. Keep your neck relaxed and continue to breathe. You may find that you are unable to perform a continuous descent, suddenly dropping all the way down halfway through the movement. This will improve with practice, but in the meantime be sure to protect your head and neck on the way down.

Glamor factor. Add load to the movement by holding a weight plate or medicine ball against your chest, being sure to keep your elbows pointing straight out to the side as you do so. Performing the movement more slowly, increasing repetitions, and/or increasing sets will also augment the impact of the exercise. While developing a well-defined six-pack is not in itself detrimental for your singing, it can restrict your breathing if you fail to stretch adequately and/or build balanced strength throughout your abdominal muscles and core. Take it slowly, and be mindful of the impact your abdominal routine has on your breathing and vocalizing.

Crunches on the go. Perform your crunches on a mat rather than on a stability ball. Lie on your back on a mat with your feet flat on the floor, heels close to your buttocks and knees up. Place your fingertips behind your ears and point your elbows straight out to the side. Keeping your neck relaxed, curl your spine up off the floor one vertebra at a time, starting with the upper back and moving down, bringing your lower ribs as close to the pelvis as possible in the front. Return nearly all the way to the starting position by uncurling your spine, making contact with the mat one vertebra at a time without releasing the tension completely, then reverse the movement and curl back up.

Figure 6.45 Stability ball crunch starting position. *Daniel Welch.*

Figure 6.46 Stability ball crunch movement. *Daniel Welch.*

Figure 6.47 Stability ball crunch end position. *Daniel Welch.*

Cardiorespiratory Training

Any activity that sustains an elevated heart rate for a period of time will improve your overall level of cardiorespiratory fitness. It's important to choose an activity you enjoy—one that makes you feel good and provides you with enough of a challenge to stay engaged without causing frustration or intolerable discomfort. Walking, running, cycling, and swimming, as well as any cardio machine available at your gym, are all terrific for improving your stroke volume and oxygen consumption.

You can tailor your regimen to boost oxygen consumption by engaging in interval training. Interval training is an approach to cardiorespiratory exercise that involves repeatedly alternating levels of intensity. For example, you could walk briskly for five minutes, jog at a faster pace for five minutes, and repeat the cycle a number of times. When you alternately challenge your heart and then allow it to cool down, it encourages your body to adapt so that you are able to meet intensity challenges more easily and recover from them more swiftly.

It is helpful to identify and target specific heart rate zones for yourself and keep track of your heart rate while performing intervals rather than just depending on a subjective sense of exercise intensity. You can track your heart rate using a heart rate monitor or one of many available devices designed to go around your wrist. Here is a simple equation for determining your target heart rate zones:

Subtract your age from 220. The result represents your maximum heart rate. Use this result to calculate your heart rate within the following three zones:

- Zone 1, 65%–75% of maximum, improves overall aerobic ability.

- Zone 2, 76%–85% of maximum, increases endurance.

- Zone 3, 86%–95% of maximum, builds aerobic capacity and stamina.

If I subtract my age, 53, from 220, my resulting maximum heart rate is 166. I can then multiply this number by the percentages required for each zone to find my recommended ranges. For example, $167 \times 65\% = 109$; $167 \times 75\% = 125$. If I wish to keep my cardio within Zone 1, I will sustain my heart rate between 109 and 125 beats per minute.

Interval training sessions of fifteen to twenty minutes, two to three times a week, often yield a swift improvement in oxygen consumption. Using the ranges you calculated for Zones 1 and 3, start off by alternating intervals of one to two minutes at each level of intensity. Begin by elevating your heart rate up to your Zone 1 parameters, and sustain it for one or two minutes; then push yourself until your heart rate enters Zone 3 and try to sustain it for one to two minutes; if this feels too uncomfortable, sustain it for as long as you can, as this can take some getting used to. Then allow your heart rate to cool back down into Zone 1 range; sustain it for one to two minutes, and continue alternating.

———————

Complete Vocal Fitness

When I began offering anatomy and fitness workshops for voice departments and conferences, the first question I'd receive from voice teachers was usually "What should we do?"

They wanted a workout program that all their students could follow. For a long while I was reluctant to design one, given the importance of customized program design. I wanted to provide each singer with a specific routine that would bring *their* unique instrument into balance.

Then it occurred to me that I could teach the singers themselves to do the customizing.

You don't have to be a certified fitness trainer to perform the simple self-assessments included in chapter 1. Just follow the guidelines to figure out where you are tight and where you are weak; then choose those stretches and exercises from the assortment presented in this chapter that will best meet your needs.

You may find that you would still benefit from some instruction and motivation, in which case any trainer who holds similar qualifications to mine will be able to help you, particularly if you share this book with him or her. I also hope that more voice departments will add fitness resources to their curricula, and I hope that those at universities with strong athletics programs explore collaboration possibilities.

The exercises presented in this chapter have been selected to help you embark on your fitness journey. Once you do, I hope you find it as enriching as I have.

7

Warming Up

Warming up my voice used to be an arduous and lengthy process. I believed that I could only adequately ready myself to perform a recital or a role by singing through the entire recital or role, hoping that enough energy and stamina would remain to get me through the actual performance. For me, the point of my warm-up was to test how well my voice was functioning. It felt fateful, like consulting my horoscope about forces beyond my ability to influence: Will I be able to sing in tune today? Will my high notes come out? Will my scales move fast enough? Will I get through those longer phrases without running out of breath? The only way to assure myself that I was ready to perform was to do a comprehensive test run. It would leave me exhausted, often also with wounded confidence about anything that hadn't gone as well as I would wish.

I know plenty of singers whose warm-up rituals consist of vocalizing along with a recording of a recent voice lesson. While more useful than my old routine, this procedure also does not stem from a place of agency and confidence because they thus place their trust not in themselves but in the opinions expressed by a teacher about how their voice was functioning at some point in the past—perhaps a few days earlier, perhaps a few months. For them, the point of the warm-up is an attempt to replicate sounds that previously earned the validation of someone they respect.

The best warm-up routine for a singer is neither one designed to assess how well your voice is functioning on a given day nor one that you believe will help you earn your teacher's validation. While such assessments may provide some good benchmarks, they are only useful within the context of a procedure that can actually *get* your voice functioning better and *raise* your performance to meet a high standard.

A truly effective warm-up routine is one that takes you from where you are to where you need to be in order to perform your best—a means to prepare your body, prime your vocal technical coordination, and center your mind.

Warming Up Your Body

Athletes engage in preperformance warm-up routines designed to increase blood flow in order to improve the suppleness and responsiveness of muscles and tendons—to literally heat themselves up. Raising the temperature of musculature through stretching and/or aerobic exercise decreases viscous resistance between layers of muscle so that muscle groups move more smoothly and easily across each other. For singers, an increase in warmth confers greater mobility not only upon large muscle groups such as those involved in breathing, but also upon the intrinsic and extrinsic muscles of the larynx. A physical warm-up of appropriate length and intensity can thus prepare the voice itself for engaging in warm-up exercises.

Athletic warm-up regimens are designed to meet the specific flexibility and strength requirements of a given sport. A physical warm-up routine for singers should include strategies to release and stretch the musculature involved in breathing, including self-myofascial release of the shoulders (figure 6.1) and stretches for the lats (figure 6.7) and pecs (figure 6.8). A short aerobic session of low to moderate intensity will encourage more expansive breathing and condition the body to meet an increase in oxygen demand. An abbreviated core strengthening routine will enliven the musculature required for stabilizing movement and breath management.

The amount of time and level of intensity you invest in the physical portion of your warm-up depends upon your unique needs. Remember that the goal is to take you from where you are to where you need to be to perform your best, so take inventory of what it will take to get you ready. If your day's activities already have you feeling flexible and energized, you need not do as much to prepare your body for singing; if you just spent four hours studying in the library, your body will need a more vigorous wake-up call. However, it is usually unwise to engage in a highly challenging physical workout on a performance day, as doing so may overly tax your musculature and deplete your energy stores.

Take inventory of your physical tensions and level of vitality, develop strategies to generate the supple liveliness you need to sing your best, and keep track of the level and types of activities that precede your best performances.

Warming Up Your Instrument

Instrumentalists warm up to reintegrate their bodies with their instrument and rehabituate the movements they execute while playing. While you may not have to perform exercises to reintegrate yourself with an external object, you face a similar transition because throughout the day your respiratory system, throat, and articulatory anatomy perform many functions other than music making. An effective warm-up enables you to home in on the specific aspects of respiration, laryngeal function, and articulation that feature in your singing.

The way your body is feeling and functioning determines the kind of physical warm-up you need; similarly, the state of your breathing, phonatory, and articulatory anatomy at the beginning of your warm-up should dictate the routine that will most effectively prepare you for performance. You must accomplish the following transitions:

Breathing. From unconscious and relatively shallow to intentional, expansive, and well modulated.

Phonation. From relatively weighty and variably focused within a restrictive pitch and dynamic range, to accessing your full pitch and dynamic range, registration potential, and consistent clarity.

Articulation. From habitual speech movements to optimal engagement and coordination of the jaw, tongue, lips, and soft palate.

Your warm-up need not take very long to accomplish all of these transitions. A few wide-ranging scales and sustained passages may be all that you need to meet these goals, as long as they provide an opportunity to assess and integrate your breathing, phonation, and articulation. The exercises you regularly perform in the service of technical development can likely be adapted for an effective warm-up routine, and you can allow a tried-and-true instrumental approach to warming up to serve as your template.

Wind and string players generally warm up in accordance with these steps:

Sustained tones to engage the generator. String players do this by bowing open strings, wind and brass players by sustaining long low notes.

Diatonic scale passages, slow and fast, within limited and then extended ranges, to activate the full pitch range and promote flexibility.

Sustained arpeggios to equalize intervals and promote consistent tone generation while changing pitches.

Melodic études to integrate generation and vibration skills with one another, as well as expressive intent.

Singers should incorporate some articulator work with scales and arpeggios and substitute phrases from repertoire for études. Be ever mindful of your purpose, which is to engage in movements and awaken your skill set rather than to assess the sounds you are making.

Vocal warm-ups should be as economical as possible. Sing only as much as necessary to prepare your voice for performance and refrain from doing anything that could lead to fatigue.

Warming Up Your Mind

In chapter 5, I pointed out that it is your intention, rather than your breath, that is the true generator of the voice. Successful, satisfying performances rest on your ability to allow expressive intent to motivate your singing. Your warm-up routine should therefore include a means of leading your mind to a state of deeper focus and concentration. This will empower you to train your full attention on your artistry and redirect your thoughts should they stray in the direction of self-criticism or other anxieties.

Any practice that sharpens your focus will enhance your performance, and any activity or phenomenon can serve as an object of meditation, so there are many different ways to design a mental warm-up procedure. Both your physical and vocal warm-ups can double as a mental warm-up if they enable you to organize your thoughts and sharpen your focus.

Assessing and acknowledging *what* you need to become centered and focused is more important than specifying *how* you will meet that need.

- Do impending performances tend to rev you up or shut you down?

- How likely are you to experience performance anxiety? How long before a performance do you expect it to set in?

- What kinds of things are liable to distract you, and how likely are you to encounter them in the context of a given production?

- How well prepared are you and your colleagues?

The prospect of going onstage may fill you with excitement, in which case you will benefit from a routine that will ground you and slow you down a bit. If instead it inclines you to space out, however, a calming meditation session will not be nearly as useful as some vigorous physical activity for mobilizing your body and mind.

If you grapple with performance anxiety, it is important not only that you devise a routine that will keep you mentally centered before and during performances but also that you initiate this routine before you are likely to feel an onset of anxiety. Engage in strategies to help manage your state prior to carrying out the physical and vocal components of your warm-up, and seek resources to diminish your anxiety symptoms for the long term.

While some distractions cannot be anticipated, many can. If you know that you will share a dressing room with a chatty colleague or that your extended family will descend on you in the hours leading up to your performance, carve out not only time but also physical space in which to center your mind.

Your degree of mental focus is likely to be proportional to your level of preparation. Even the most disciplined singer may occasionally have to perform without being as fully prepared as he or she would wish, perhaps when filling in for an ailing colleague on short notice or due to last-minute staging changes. This means an increase in the mental demands of your job because in addition to your singing you must keep track of extra things like new blocking or unfamiliar text. You will need to increase your focus proportionally in order to meet these demands, as well as to contend with any increase in stress caused by the situation.

There is no universal warm-up protocol that would suit all singers under every circumstance. Even the order in which one warms up the body, voice, and mind will differ in accordance with personal preference. I find that focusing my mind first makes the rest of my warm-up more effective, and that warming up my body leaves me well-prepared to vocalize—but your experience may differ. The amount of time required for the individual components of your warm-up may vary for you on different days. Get in the habit of taking inventory of your physical, vocal, and mental state; measuring the distance between where you are and where you need to be; and allotting adequate time and resources for a comprehensive warm-up every time you perform.

Once a performance begins, there are many things that are beyond your control. However, contrary to what I once believed, how you prepare yourself to give your best performance is something that *is* within your control. Settle your mind, warm up your body, vocalize intelligently, and you will never have to wonder whether your voice will function well. You will know just what steps to take to ensure that it does.

8

Fueling Your Art

Sports nutritionists look at food as an energy source. They conduct detailed analyses of the activities athletes engage in throughout their day in order to help them meet the energy requirements of training and performance. Whatever an athlete's short- and long-term goals—increased muscle mass, a leaner profile, improved endurance, or greater explosive power—the nutritionists who serve them create dietary protocols fine-tuned to support their achievement.

These protocols prescribe the nutritional composition, caloric content, and timing of meals and snacks. They are designed to promote not only effective performance but also recovery following a training session or event. In addition to providing student athletes robust support from staff nutritionists, an increasing number of schools with NCAA athletics programs now offer access to "fueling stations" stocked with energy-rich foods throughout the morning and afternoon to make it easier for students to comply with nutrition protocols.

Such resources would also hold tremendous benefit for the health and success of voice performance majors. Like other athletes, singers must simultaneously cultivate bodies capable of specialized energy expenditure while continually fueling their bodies for training and performance. But even if we do not have a team of nutritionists to help us meet our metabolic requirements, we can study the protocols developed on behalf of student athletes and adapt them to meet our needs.

Most of the guidelines that registered dieticians and sports nutritionists draw on are available to fitness trainers as well as all other laymen. For example, the nutrition guidelines that the Food and Drug Administration (FDA) publishes are an outstanding publicly available resource. They serve as my primary reference for much of what follows.

The Essential Building Blocks

Nutrients vary in their efficiency for fueling different categories of activities, so we must familiarize ourselves with the types of nutrients we consume and the roles they play in our biochemistry; it is also important to consider how each nutrient can best be sourced.

Most foods that humans consume break down into three categories of macronutrients: carbohydrates, proteins, and lipids. I will discuss the fuel efficiency of each macronutrient and criteria for evaluating their qualities.

Carbohydrates

Most carbohydrates come from plant sources, with the exception of the lactose found in dairy products. Carbohydrates include sugars, starches, and dietary fiber. During digestion sugars and starches are broken down into glucose, our primary fuel source. Dietary fiber promotes satiety and regulates digestion. Carbohydrates contain four calories per gram. The FDA recommends that carbohydrates make up 45 percent to 65 percent of your daily caloric intake.

Whole grains, fresh fruits, and vegetables are excellent sources of carbohydrates. They contain healthy quantities of dietary fiber and naturally occurring vitamins and minerals. Processed foods containing added sugars and refined grains are considered less nutritious and less fuel-efficient due to a lack of dietary fiber, vitamins, and minerals, as well as a higher relative caloric content.

Proteins

Proteins are found in a wide variety of plant and animal sources, including legumes, dairy products, meat, poultry, fish, and shellfish, as well as some grains and vegetables. Like carbohydrates, proteins are a source of fuel, vitamins, and minerals. In addition, protein provides us with the nine essential amino acids required for building and repairing cells, immune response, hormone production, and many other bodily functions. Proteins contain four calories per gram. The FDA recommends that proteins make up 10 percent to 35 percent of your daily caloric intake.

Animal and soy proteins are called "complete proteins," because they provide all nine essential amino acids our bodies require in balanced amounts. Most plant protein sources are considered "incomplete proteins," because they are either missing certain essential amino acids or do not contain them in adequate quantity. However, two or more plant proteins can complement each other and serve as a complete protein—for example, legumes and grains consumed together can provide all the essential amino acids. Vegetarians must take care to ensure their diets provide adequate protein.

Both animal and plant protein sources can contain a significant quantity of fat, the third macronutrient. Seek protein sources that are rich in nutrients and low in fat, such as legumes, soy products, poultry, fish, and lean meats. Like carbohydrates, fresh protein sources are likely to be higher in nutrients than processed foods.

Lipids (Fats)

Like proteins, fats are found in a wide variety of plant and animal sources. In addition to providing the body with fuel, fat serves as a component of cell membranes, protects internal organs, assists in the absorption of vitamins, and supports many other bodily functions. Fats contribute to a sense of satiety and contain nine calories per gram. The FDA recommends that fats make up 20 percent to 35 percent of your daily caloric intake.

There are two types of fat. Saturated fat is usually solid at room temperature and comes primarily from animal sources. Unsaturated fat is usually liquid at room temperature and comes primarily from plant sources. Trans fat is a type of unsaturated fat that has been partially hydrogenated and should be avoided due to its harmful impact on cholesterol levels.

Because fats contain more than twice the caloric content of carbohydrates and proteins, it can be challenging to limit your fat intake to 20 percent to 35 percent of your daily caloric intake. Seek lean protein sources and fresh produce, and read the labels on processed foods carefully. Prioritize unsaturated fats when possible, as excessive consumption of saturated fats can raise your LDL cholesterol level and increase your risk of cardiovascular disease.

Calculating Your Energy Requirements

Everything our bodies do requires continuous, reliable sources of energy. Not only our biomechanics but also cognition, blood circulation, and even the digestive process itself depend on the ability to access quality fuel in order to function properly.

How many calories an individual needs on a daily basis depends on a number of variables, including age, weight, gender, body composition, activity level, and genetics. While a thorough medical evaluation is necessary to determine your daily caloric expenditure with any precision, the Harris-Benedict equation to determine basal metabolic rate (BMR) can provide an excellent estimate:

- For men, BMR = 66 + (6.2 × weight in pounds) + (12.7 × height in inches) – (6.76 × age in years)

- For women, BMR = 655.1 + (4.35 × weight in pounds) + (4.7 × height in inches) – (4.7 × age in years)

Your BMR reflects the number of calories your body needs to continue functioning while completely at rest. At the time of this writing I am 53 years old, 63 inches tall and weigh 150 pounds. If I plug these numbers into the Harris-Benedict equation, I find that I need a minimum of 1,350 calories each day in order to just do things like breathe, circulate my blood, think, and maintain a healthy body temperature. In order to calculate the total daily calories I am likely to expend, I will have to factor in my body composition and activity level. To estimate your daily caloric needs, multiply your BMR by the number corresponding to your usual activity level:

- Little to no exercise: BMR × 1.2

- Light exercise (1–3 days per week): BMR × 1.375

- Moderate exercise (3–5 days per week): BMR × 1.55

- Heavy exercise (6–7 days per week): BMR × 1.725

- Very heavy exercise (twice per day, extra-heavy workouts): BMR × 1.9

I engage in heavy exercise, so I will multiply my BMR by 1.725 for a result of 2,330; I can confirm that on a typically active day that is about the number of calories I must consume in order to feel physically competent and energetic.

An estimation of your daily caloric needs is helpful for creating dietary strategies to effectively fuel your workouts and performances. Once you have this estimate, you'll need to distribute it among the meals and snacks you consume throughout the day and decide how many calories from carbohydrates, proteins, and fats should compose each. With the right tools and some practice, you will find that this is less complicated than it sounds. Online resources abound to help you determine the caloric and nutritional content of most foods, and smartphone apps like LoseIt! incorporate bar code scanners that display nutritional information for commercially packaged items. Invest in a kitchen scale to measure portions of fresh produce.

Fueling Workouts and Performances

Glucose is the body's primary energy source, so your preworkout snack or meal should provide you with adequate carbohydrates to fuel your exercise and maintain blood sugar levels. Choose carbohydrates with a middle to low glycemic index, such as whole grains, fresh fruits, and vegetables. The glycemic index ranks carbohydrates in terms of how quickly they break down and enter the bloodstream as glucose. Carbohydrates with a lower glycemic index, such as whole grains, are processed more slowly by our bodies and therefore provide a steadier, more sustainable source of fuel; those with a high glycemic index, such as the high-fructose corn syrup often found in soft drinks, provide an energy spike that swiftly fizzles.

Proteins are effective for aiding postworkout muscle recovery and growth. Proteins are best processed and absorbed by your body when your protein intake is distributed fairly evenly between meals rather than taken in a single large infusion either right after a workout (a popular myth with athletes) or at dinnertime (characteristic of the typical American diet).

Fats have not been shown to have a significant impact on either performance or recovery and therefore can be consumed in proportion to other nutrients throughout the day.

It's important to stay adequately hydrated for both workouts and performances. This means maintaining a fluid balance in the body that is sufficient for regulating body temperature. Physical exertion generates heat (literally the result of burning calories), and sweat production cools the body down. Drink water or a sports performance beverage continuously throughout your workout to replenish your body's fluid balance, ensure efficient heat distribution, and avoid overheating. How much fluid is necessary to maintain balance depends on exercise intensity and differs from person to person. Do not wait until you feel thirsty to take a drink, as a sensation of thirst indicates a degree of fluid loss that is already having a negative impact on your performance.

In many ways, the nutritional needs of athletes do not differ significantly from those of nonathletes. We each have a specific daily caloric requirement that will keep us healthy and high-functioning, to be met with a balance of carbohydrates (45%–65%), proteins (10%–35%), and fats (20%–35%). The most significant difference between the way athletes and nonathletes eat has to do with timing and distribution of macronutrients throughout the day:

- Consume carbohydrates prior to exercise in sufficient quantity to sustain adequate glycogen levels to fuel the workout.

- Consume a balance of carbohydrates and protein postexercise to restore blood sugar levels and facilitate recovery.

- Divide total protein consumption over several meals rather than consuming it in a single infusion.

- Plan the timing and content of meals and snacks to meet the energy demands of specific physical activities. At times this will mean distributing daily caloric content over five or more meals, some of which may not fall at socially conventional times.

Here is how my 2,340-calorie meal plan might look on an active day that begins with a workout and ends with a performance.

7:30 A.M.: PREWORKOUT MEAL, 275 CALORIES

Oatmeal with sliced banana. The calories from carbohydrates roughly equal what I will burn in a typical strength-training workout.

9:30 A.M.: WORKOUT RECOVERY/BREAKFAST, 400 CALORIES

Egg white scramble with fresh vegetables and feta cheese and a slice of whole-grain toast. Carbs to restore blood sugar and protein to help with muscle recovery.

1:00 P.M.: LUNCH, 630 CALORIES

Brown rice bowl with stir-fried chicken and root vegetables. A balance of complex carbohydrates and lean protein.

4:30 P.M.: SNACK, 175 CALORIES

Apple slices and toasted almonds. I'll need a snack to keep me from feeling so famished that I wolf down my preperformance meal and end up with digestive discomfort.

6:30 P.M.: PREPERFORMANCE MEAL, 450 CALORIES

Linguini tossed with olive oil, pine nuts, and parmesan. I personally prefer normal pasta made with refined flour to whole-grain varieties. Whole-grain pasta has a higher glycemic index and would provide me with a slower, more sustainable energy source, but the fiber is more challenging to digest. The fat and protein from the oil, nuts, and cheese will help with satiety and provide nutrients that will take a bit longer to enter my bloodstream. This meal might not work as well for someone else, but it leaves me feeling full and comfortable enough to get through a recital.

10:00 P.M.: PERFORMANCE RECOVERY, 400 CALORIES

Whatever is on hand at the reception that looks the most like lean protein, consumed in moderation. A couple of chicken skewers or smoked salmon canapés will do the trick.

Postperformance Perils

As important as it is to fuel a performance well, it is perhaps even more vital that you plan for your recovery. The best preperformance meal may still leave you starving by the time the show wraps up. It's late at night, and you'll likely find yourself either at a reception where you'll be tempted by delicacies or at whatever comfort food restaurant is still open at that hour. What you need is a moderate serving of complex carbs and lean protein; what you're more likely to be offered is a luscious helping of saturated fat in the form of a wedge of Brie or a cheeseburger. Know yourself. If your judgment is likely to be clouded when you're hungry and faced with temptation, bring a healthy postperformance snack to be consumed prior to leaving the theater so that a feeling of satiety can buffer your resolve.

Cultural Challenges

If you look at food as an energy source, it is relatively easy to map out a regimen that provides adequate fuel and nutrition to support your overall health, as well as effective performances. All you need to do is calculate your basal metabolic rate, assess your daily caloric needs, and fulfill them with a balance of macronutrients appropriately distributed to fuel the various types of exertion in which you engage throughout the day.

However, our culture tends to view food as either a source of hedonistic gratification or a dangerous substance that continually threatens to make us obese. If eating well has become a challenge, it is not due to any mysteries surrounding nutrition but rather the ubiquitous media messages constantly exhorting us to consume things that exceed and subvert our dietary needs and the proliferation of other misleading messages telling us how to achieve an unrealistic body image. The obstacles to healthy eating include the following:

Marketing. Restaurant chains and other large food corporations profit by selling as much of their product as they can, often in the form of single meals containing more calories than you'd need over the course of an entire day.

Proliferation of processed and hyperpalatable foods. It's cheaper and more expedient to eat highly processed packaged foods full of sodium, preservatives, and artificial flavoring than it is to buy and prepare fresh, nutrient-rich produce. And while we now inhabit a highly functioning civilization that facilitates fairly sedentary lives, we have not yet evolved beyond craving the quantities of fat, carbs, and salt we once needed to be effective hunter-gatherers without heated homes.

The diet industry. The US Department of Health and Human Services currently estimates that two-thirds of American adults are overweight or obese; meanwhile, our media concurrently promote ideals of thinness that are unachievable for most healthy people. Thus there are countless corporations offering supplements and diet plans that trade on the despair of a population seeking an unattainable physical aesthetic without being able to facilitate lasting results.

Short-term compensatory psychological gains of over- or undereating. Eating disorders are difficult to treat. Sixty percent of people with eating disorders who receive treatment are thought to make a full recovery; without treatment, up to 20 percent of people with serious eating disorders will die.

Arguably the biggest obstacle to developing healthy eating habits is our culture's tendency to focus on physical appearance rather than on function, and a resulting obsession with weight management. This is an issue that athletes struggle with as well. Coaches will sometimes admonish athletes to lose weight in order to achieve a profile more advantageous for their area of specialization, failing to realize that such weight loss, if pursued incorrectly, may end up being quite detrimental to their performance. Sports nutritionists counsel athletes and their trainers to focus on improving their weight-to-strength ratio rather than on weight loss. Improving overall body composition yields a slimmer profile because it leads to an increase in lean muscle mass and a decrease in body fat, and muscle tissue occupies roughly one-third the volume of fat tissue by weight. Conversely, weight loss pursued as an end in itself can lead to a decrease in muscle mass as well as dehydration—and limiting caloric intake will lead to diminished energy and stamina. This is as much a problem for an opera singer as it is for a gymnast.

In this chapter I have recommended that you calculate the daily number of calories to support your weight and exercise habits in order to design a nutrition plan that will effectively fuel your activities throughout the day. However, the discussions we tend to have about calorie consumption nearly always arise within the context of weight management, in spite of the fact that merely reducing caloric consumption rarely leads to sustainable weight loss.

The idea is that if you fail to consume adequate calories to maintain your weight, your body will be constrained to burn stored fat to make up for the food you didn't eat. But this isn't exactly how it works. It's much easier for us to produce the fuel we need from the nutrients we consume than it is for us to convert stored fat into energy. When faced with a caloric deficit, our bodies may instead attempt to conserve the energy we have, resulting in both physical and mental fatigue and potentially slowing down our metabolism long-term so that we burn fewer calories by default. While weight loss can only be achieved by creating a caloric deficit, the best strategy for creating this deficit appears to be through strategies that boost your metabolism (so that you're burning more calories daily by default) while moderately reducing caloric intake to a level where you can still fuel your activities appropriately and avoid sending your body into conservation mode.

My advice for singers is that you adopt a diet and exercise regimen designed to sustain your energy throughout the day while optimizing your body for peak performance. Unless your doctor has recommended that you lose weight for health reasons, I encourage you to view weight management as a secondary goal. Weight-loss diet plans often propose drastically unrealistic caloric deficits. According to the Harris-Benedict principle, I need about 1,350 calories daily simply to stay alive and functioning, so you can see that the 1,200-calorie limit frequently recommended for weight loss isn't enough for me to just get through the day, let alone excel in the gym or concert hall!

Be extremely wary of anyone hawking supplements that promise swift metabolic boosts, muscle gain, or weight loss. Registered dieticians advocate reliance on whole foods for nutrition and exercise extreme rigor when recommending even the most basic vitamin and mineral supplements;

sports nutritionists find themselves perpetually combatting myths propagated by for-profit supplement producers. Reputable fitness certification programs require trainers who complete these programs to provide only advice that falls within the scope of their practice rather than professing expertise in medicine, biochemistry, and so on. Certification as a fitness trainer does not represent any specialized qualifications in the area of nutrition, so a trainer peddling supplements is just a salesman in sweats, not a diet expert.

Food is far more than an energy source. It can also of course be a source of tremendous pleasure. Like most creative artists, I am a hedonist at heart, and I encourage you to indulge your appetite for sensual gratification alongside your need for effective fuel and balanced nutrition. All you really need to devise and comply with healthy dietary principles is a little knowledge and the willingness to set a high priority on the needs of your instrument and your craft.

9

Maintaining Your Health

A clarinetist I performed with as a high school student later endured a miserable first semester as a conservatory freshman. She had been accepted into the studio of a phenomenal teacher at a prestigious school. While she knew that working with him would mean major changes to her embouchure and overall technique, she still seemed incapable of producing a focused, resonant sound after several months of practice. Even her new teacher began to express concern.

Then she brought her clarinet to the repair shop for a tune-up and discovered that she had been playing on an instrument impaired by a significant but invisible crack. The problem had never been her embouchure—her instrument had been malfunctioning.

One of the reasons that I feel it is so important for singers to understand how your instrument functions is so that when a problem arises, you can discern whether it is an issue of skill or physiology and pursue an effective solution based on that information. If you understand how your voice ought to respond when it is healthy, it becomes easier to recognize when a medical issue is interfering with your singing. Conversely, if it is always a mystery whether your voice will work on a given day, you are likely to develop the chronic hypochondriacal angst so common to our profession.

The most impeccable technique is unfortunately not always sufficient to keep hypochondria at bay. Paranoia about health is rampant in our community, and the strategies singers adopt to avoid getting sick are as far-ranging and idiosyncratic as our voices. So pervasive is this problem that Peter Gelb, general manager of the Metropolitan Opera, reportedly once went so far as to consider commissioning a study to catalog the maladies responsible for company member cancellations.

Such a study would be pointless because as a class, singers are in fact no more vulnerable to illness than the average human. Our paranoid tendencies arise from the simple truth that the professional consequences are far more extreme for us than they are for almost anyone else when we do get sick.

For any given profession, there is a baseline level of health and energy required to perform one's job well. I would argue that the level of health and energy necessary for adequate performance as a classical singer is higher than for nearly any other occupation. A head cold will not prevent a lawyer or an accountant from turning in a fine day's work. A dental hygienist can don a face mask and continue attending to patients. Even news anchors or talk-show hosts with a touch of the flu can show up to work, because even if their audiences perceive some hoarseness in their speaking voices, they will be forgiven because they are, after all, human. But a classical singer will not be forgiven if the symptoms of a head cold or flu impact your tone, narrow your range, or cause a phlegmy rattle on certain pitches. When successfully doing our job requires us to maintain perfect health at all times, it's no wonder that those for whom the stakes are nowhere near as high view us as hypochondriacs.

Another reason for our paranoia around health issues is that a singer who is not healthy enough to perform may receive no pay for weeks of work they have already put in. Opera companies commonly offer contracts providing payment for performances rather than guaranteeing a fee that covers rehearsal weeks. In such a case, a singer who devotes several weeks to preparation but then becomes too sick to go on takes a crushing financial hit. Throughout this book I have argued that we are as much athletes as we are artists, but even professional athletes do not face dire consequences for canceling an event due to illness or injury. An NFL linebacker will not find his multiyear contract canceled for missing a couple of games due to bronchitis; an Olympic skater will not lose corporate sponsorship while recovering from an ankle sprain. But an opera singer who cancels a performance due to illness is likely to forfeit a huge percentage of his or her expected earnings . . . and prompt the general manager of the company to consider studying why we are so much more susceptible to medical issues than it seems we ought to be.

Athletic culture is aware that everyone succumbs to illness or injury from time to time; opera culture views illness as unforgivable.

Singers are thus under tremendous pressure to remain healthy. Our employers depend on it, and our personal financial well-being relies on it. The paranoia this can instill makes us that much more susceptible to anyone marketing a magic pill to guard us against illness. There are no end of herbal supplements, tinctures, and teas that promise a bulletproof immune system. There is a strong temptation to confer with your colleagues, each of whom has their preferred elixir, and to fall down the rabbit hole of adding everything they recommend to an increasingly complex and expensive daily regimen that may do nothing at all to fortify your health, further escalating your sense of paranoia and vulnerability.

I therefore offer two general guidelines for getting through a singing career with a reasonable degree of physical and mental health:

1. Pursue only those strategies for staying healthy that are supported by medical and scientific knowledge, rather than relying on anecdotal advice from colleagues.

2. Understand that even if you do absolutely everything within your power to stay healthy, you will still occasionally get sick.

Singers do not get sick at a different rate than nonsingers. The strategies that doctors recommend to keep normal people healthy can serve us extremely well, as long as we acknowledge how imperative it is for us to follow them consistently.

Best Practices for Staying Healthy

As I discussed in chapter 8, the education that fitness trainers receive emphasizes the importance of only providing advice that is well within the scope of our practice. We are qualified to offer exercise instruction and perform basic first-aid interventions when called upon, but we are not medical professionals. In my opinion, voice teachers should be similarly mindful of our scope of practice and refrain from dispensing medical advice. Therefore, the suggestions provided in this section reflect widely available medical research as opposed to my own expertise.

Wash Your Hands Frequently.

Keep your hands clean. We frequently come into contact with potentially harmful germs just in the course of day-to-day living. Exposure to raw meat, a colleague with a cold, and countless other things can put us in contact with something potentially infectious, and anything that gets on your hands can end up inside your body when you touch your eyes, nose, or mouth. Hand washing has been shown to prevent up to 20 percent of respiratory infections. The Food and Drug Administration finds that plain soap and warm water is sufficient for keeping your hands germ-free, so there is no need to hold out for antibacterial soap or the perfect hand-sanitizing gel. Wash your hands.

Get Adequate Sleep.

Adults require from seven to nine hours of sleep nightly to support their health and energy levels. Sleep deficiency can compromise your immune system, making you more vulnerable to viruses and infection; it also increases your risk for heart disease, kidney disease, diabetes, and obesity. In addition to supporting your physical health, adequate sleep promotes optimal brain function, improving your abilities to retain new learning and make effective decisions. Rather than burning the midnight oil to memorize your score or plot your next career move, get a good night's rest. You'll improve your productivity as well as your chances of maintaining your health.

Drink Enough Water.

As I discussed in chapter 8, proper hydration is essential for your health and physical functioning. Water regulates body temperature, eliminates toxins, and protects joints and tissues. Optimal water intake will vary for each individual. The National Institutes of Health guidelines recommend 3,000 ml daily for adult men and 2,200 ml for women, but there is no need to obsessively measure your fluid intake. If you drink enough water throughout the day to avoid becoming uncomfortably thirsty, you are probably keeping yourself adequately hydrated. Singers do not need to drink a greater quantity of water than average people.

Don't Smoke.

Smoking is detrimental for classical singing in a number of significant ways.

- *Smoking causes coughing.* The chemicals in cigarettes damage the cilia in our trachea, preventing them from catching inhaled toxins before they can enter the lungs and necessitating that we cough in order to clear the toxins out again. Coughing can be highly traumatic for the vocal folds and must be avoided when possible.

- *Smoking irritates your vocal folds.* Smoking dries the vocal folds, prompting a buildup of mucus in the area. It can also cause inflammation that thickens the vocal folds, lowering the pitch and diminishing control over registration.

- *Smoking irreversibly impairs pulmonary function.* Smoking damages the alveoli, the air sacs in the lungs that exchange carbon dioxide for oxygen. As I explained in chapter 2, our ability to sustain long phrases depends far more on oxygen satiety than on lung capacity, so diminished oxygen intake will lead to diminished breath management for singing.

Additionally, the surgeon general finds that smoking causes lung cancer, heart disease, and myriad other ailments that could prove problematic for your singing career.

Maintain Adequate Humidity While Sleeping.

Breathing in dry air overnight can desiccate the skin of your nasal passages and throat, causing minuscule cracks that leave you more vulnerable to bacterial and viral infection. Just as cigarette smoke damages the cilia in your lungs, dry air can damage the cilia of the nasal and sinus cavities, limiting their ability to guard your airways against toxins. Use a hygrometer to monitor the humidity in your bedroom and run a humidifier overnight when necessary. Aim for 40 percent to 50 percent humidity during warmer months; in colder months, maintain the highest humidity level you can without allowing condensation to form on your windows, as too humid an environment can promote bacterial growth. If you find that you are unable to keep the humidity over 20 percent due either to excessive dryness or risk of condensation, spend some quality time with a steam inhaler upon waking.

Use a Saline Nasal Rinse Daily.

A saline rinse washes away thickened mucus and toxins, helps keep the nasal passages open, reduces postnasal drip, and promotes healthy cilia. It keeps the area clean and moist, and it can flush out germs before they have an opportunity to cause an infection. Combine a premeasured salt packet designed specifically for this use with the prescribed quantity of distilled or boiled water, not tap water. Either a neti pot or a squeeze bottle will do the trick.

Protect Yourself during Air Travel.

From a health standpoint, air travel is taxing in numerous ways. The air in the cabin is pressurized to mimic high-elevation conditions; it contains a smaller quantity of oxygen, which would be present at high elevation and is also quite dry. These conditions make it difficult to sleep and stay adequately hydrated, and the recirculation of air through the cabin enables passengers for whom optimal health is not a high priority to share their germs with you. It is up to you to mitigate these adverse conditions as best you can. Wearing a surgical mask will protect you from stray germs; wearing a HumidiFlyer will help keep you hydrated. Keep plenty of water handy—pick up a big bottle once you are through security, or pack an empty bottle that you can fill before boarding in case bottled water is not available on the other side. Do your best to plan travel so as to avoid having to fly and then sing later that same day. If you have an audition, fly the previous night and sleep in a hotel. If you're on tour and have to perform on consecutive days in different cities, catching a red-eye flight after a show so that you can sleep and wake up in the location where you will next perform will likely leave you better rejuvenated than having to travel and perform in a new location.

Keep Current with Immunizations.

The Centers for Disease Control and Prevention recommend that all adults be vaccinated annually for influenza, every ten years for tetanus, and once for chicken pox. Other vaccinations may be recommended depending upon age and individual risk factors. Schedule a flu shot each year as soon as it becomes available, and ask your doctor whether there are additional immunizations he or she recommends. You will almost certainly be exposed to people who already have the flu because it isn't nearly as important for them as it is for you to avoid catching it or to stay home while they recover. Protect yourself.

Be Smart about Alcohol Consumption.

If drinking is something you enjoy, get to know the way your body and mind generally respond to alcohol. Establish guidelines for yourself and follow them to ensure that drinking never poses a problem for your singing.

Don't drink on the job. Classical singing demands your very best physical and mental coordination, and a small amount of alcohol will impair your motor control and cognitive abilities to some extent. Alcohol also causes dehydration, which will have a negative impact on vocal function. Never drink before a coaching, rehearsal, or performance. While alcohol may reliably settle your nerves in social settings, drinking is not an effective way to contend with performance anxiety.

Don't do the crime if you can't do the time. In addition to poor coordination and dehydration, heavy drinking can lead to nausea, acid reflux, headaches, and difficulty sleeping. Know your limits and avoid drinking beyond your ability to recover in time for a rehearsal or performance; for many singers, that may mean abstaining when you have to sing the following day. If drinking or hangover symptoms have impaired your ability to do your job on more than one occasion, seek evaluation for addiction.

Indulge intelligently. Artists tend to be hedonistic—if we don't live it up at least a little, we won't have all that much to sing about! Deprivation for its own sake will not support your health.

Speed your recovery. Hangovers result from a combination of dehydration, starvation, and shock. You can avoid or minimize these symptoms by drinking plenty of water, avoiding drinking on an empty stomach, and taking a vitamin B complex supplement prior to going to sleep.

What to Do When You *Do* Get Sick

When you find yourself with an affliction that threatens to impede your effectiveness as a singer, your two highest priorities are to get well as quickly as possible, and to ensure that your condition does not worsen to the point that it turns into something more nefarious. For example, without early intervention, a cold or flu can develop into a sinus infection; a bacterial infection can develop into a fungal infection. Best practices for both of these priorities are the same.

- If something harmful has gotten into your body and there is a medication available that will get it out of you, take that medication.

- Keep your respiratory passages open.

- If you are coughing, do what you can to stop.

- Address gastroesophageal reflux as aggressively as possible.

Medicate When Necessary.

If you have an ailment that can be alleviated by medication, acquire and administer that medication as soon as you can. Do not wait to see whether you start to feel either better or worse. If you have a bacterial infection or strep throat, the sooner you take an antibiotic the sooner you will feel better; you will also minimize the possibility that your symptoms will worsen. If you are concerned about overprescription of antibiotics, the solution is to refrain from taking them when you do not need them. If you have a bacterial infection, take them—you need them. If you catch the flu, take Tamiflu if possible. It will shorten your illness by a valuable day or two, and that can make the difference between being able to perform and having to cancel. Recovering from the flu more swiftly may also prevent you from developing a sinus infection.

Keep Your Respiratory Passages Open.

If you are experiencing nasal and/or chest congestion, pursue specific symptom relief in order to breathe adequately. Pharmaceutical companies produce quite an array of multisymptom medications, so be discerning in your selection of over-the-counter (OTC) medications and take only those that will treat the symptoms you are experiencing. Some medications in the multisymptom formulas may yield undesirable side effects such as impaired cognition or physical coordination, which will make it difficult to do your job well. If you don't need them, don't take them.

Treat Nasal Congestion.

If you have nasal congestion, take a nasal decongestant. Nasal decongestants reduce swelling by constricting blood vessels in the nasal cavities and are available in both topical and oral forms. Sudafed remains the gold standard of oral decongestants; it is available in the United States at pharmacy counters with valid identification and without a prescription. Steroid nasal sprays are available for nasal congestion resulting from a chronic condition. Consult your physician to determine whether a topical or oral decongestant or steroid nasal spray will best meet your needs.

Treat Chest Congestion.

If you have chest congestion, take an expectorant. Expectorants loosen congestion in the airways and lungs by increasing the hydration of mucous secretions, making them easier to expel. Guaifenesin, the active ingredient in Mucinex, is an expectorant that also has muscle relaxant properties and thus makes coughing both more productive and less potentially damaging to the vocal folds.

Treat a Runny Nose.

A runny nose can be annoying, but it will not necessarily keep you from singing well; however, antihistamines, which provide symptomatic relief for a runny nose, can make you feel drowsy or disoriented, compromising your coordination and alertness and making it difficult to sing. If you require antihistamines to manage allergies or are experiencing painful postnasal drip secondary to a sinus infection, work with your physician to identify the option least likely to cause excessive drowsiness. Otherwise, I recommend just blowing your nose. I also recommend avoiding multi-symptom OTC medications that include an antihistamine—treat only those symptoms that are causing you actual difficulty.

Treat Fever, Pain, and/or Inflammation.

These three symptoms often arise together. Whether and how you choose to treat all of them requires some consideration. According to a recent National Institutes of Health study, there is increasing support for allowing a low-grade fever (less than 103°F) to run its course rather than using medication to suppress it. However, if these symptoms are causing you intolerable discomfort, you have some options. Medications with acetaminophen suppress fever and relieve pain. Nonsteroidal anti-inflammatory agents (NSAIDs), which commonly include ibuprofen, suppress fever, relieve pain, *and* reduce inflammation. If singing is painful, do not take medication to make it easier to sing through the pain—allow yourself some rest.

Avoid Coughing.

If you are coughing, it is vital for the well-being of your voice that you do what you can to stop. Coughing can be traumatic to the vocal folds, potentially leading to hemorrhage or tears, so take a cough suppressant. Dextromethorphan, the most common active ingredient found in OTC cough suppressants, works by inhibiting the cough reflex, but I have personally found it to be inadequate for the needs of singers. I recommend working with your physician to identify a non-drowsy cough suppressant that will serve your needs during the day, as well as a narcotic option to help you sleep through the night without coughing. Benzonatate, the active ingredient found in the prescription cough suppressant Tessalon Perles, suppresses coughs by numbing the stretch sensors in the lungs. If you can safely take narcotic medications, Hycodan is an effective overnight cough suppressant.

Address Gastroesophageal Reflux Disease Aggressively.

Gastroesophageal reflux disease (GERD) is a chronic condition wherein partially digested food backs up into the esophagus, resulting in heartburn and exposing the vocal folds to potentially devastating stomach acid. The symptoms of GERD can often be managed by adjusting your diet to cut back on acidic foods and beverages and refraining from eating too close to bedtime; however, it's hard to be disciplined when you find yourself famished after a performance and are offered rich food and cocktails at a late-night reception. If diet and lifestyle changes are not sufficient to eliminate your symptoms, the next line of defense is medication. Proton pump inhibitors are effective for reducing stomach acid; however, as of this writing their efficacy and safety have yet to be studied for long-term use. In extreme cases, surgery is sometimes necessary to get GERD symptoms under control. If you are having reflux issues, see a gastroenterologist immediately for diagnosis and treatment.

Accessing Medical Care

This section primarily addresses the needs of U.S. residents at a moment when health insurance laws and services are in flux. However, the basic priorities expressed here hold true for singers worldwide.

It is of vital importance to acquire a health insurance policy that will facilitate swift, affordable access to an otolaryngologist whether you are performing at home, with regional companies, or abroad. Achieving this may be difficult and/or costly, but it will greatly benefit not only your health but also your peace of mind.

If you are on the road and need to see an otolaryngologist but have a health insurance policy that offers only geographically restricted areas of service, such as a health maintenance organization (HMO), you will have to go home in order to receive care. In such a case, you may have to choose between forgoing treatment and canceling your gig. If your plan potentially covers a visit to an otolaryngologist where you are working but requires a referral, that will delay your ability to access care. Ideally, what you need is a policy that offers nationwide in-network care, without a need for referrals. Most of those policies take the form of preferred provider organizations (PPOs). Such a policy will not only ensure timely access to an otolaryngologist but will also minimize the necessity of visiting an emergency room should any health issue arise while you're on the road, as you will be covered for visits to other local specialists as well. Unfortunately, not every state offers PPOs on the exchange, but you still may be able to find a policy with out-of-network coverage.

If you want ready access to an otolaryngologist when you're out of the country, then in addition to a PPO with nationwide in-network coverage you will also need a supplemental policy for international travel. Such policies are available on a per-trip basis or on an annual, renewable basis. If you will be performing abroad for an extended period of time, you may wish to look into obtaining an insurance policy from the country where you are working. Either way, seek a policy that will cover you on its own rather than first billing your primary insurance, as this will save you from a potentially overwhelming bureaucratic burden.

Primary Care

Seek a primary care physician who understands your priorities and the level of health you must maintain in order to do your job well. If you enjoy excellent rapport and develop a high level of trust with your doctor, you will feel comfortable turning to him or her when you need assistance and be accepting of his or her advice, rather than endlessly googling and self-diagnosing symptoms as they arise. The right doctor will be on the lookout for things that might not bother an ordinary person but are potentially hazardous for your career, such as medications with side effects that are detrimental to your voice or procedures that could have a long-term impact on breathing or phonation. The right doctor will help you seek options that will support rather than impair your instrument.

When to See a Doctor

The earlier you receive a diagnosis and treatment for an illness, the less it will interfere with your work. When possible, I encourage you to see your doctor as soon as you experience symptoms for which medical assistance would prove useful.

High fever. See a doctor if you have a fever of 102°F or higher and are unable to reduce it with OTC medications.

Painful sore throat. There are a number of things that can cause a painful sore throat, many of which are best resolved with a prescription medication. It's vital that you find out what is really going on and access the best possible treatment.

Thick yellow or green mucus. Mucus that is clear, white, or very pale yellow may indicate a common cold, but if it is dark yellow, green, or blood-streaked it would be wise to see your doctor to find out whether you have an infection requiring antibacterial or antifungal medication.

Persistent diarrhea. Diarrhea that lasts for two days or more puts you at risk for dehydration, among other things. Seek medical assistance to resolve it swiftly and rule out the possibility that it is symptomatic of a more serious condition.

When to Cancel

When your voice does not feel 100 percent healthy and functional, the decision of whether or not to go on can be a difficult and personal one. There are a number of factors to consider. If your singing remains competent though not transcendent and you will forfeit your paycheck by canceling, the right choice for you may be to perform. You may risk a poor review, but if you need the money and enjoy a reputation that is strong enough to survive a ding or two, you may elect to go on. However, if your voice is impaired to the point where you cannot access the range necessary to perform a role, your cords are not closing adequately to produce a focused sound, or you are coughing uncontrollably, you must cancel—not only for the sake of the production but also to avoid injuring yourself.

Be a responsible colleague and cancel rehearsals, lessons, and coachings if you have an illness that may be contagious, even if you are not presenting with symptoms that prevent you from singing.

Coping with Anesthesiology

If you need a procedure requiring general anesthesia, have a conversation with your anesthesiologist to explain your priorities and request advice. Intubation must be undertaken with care in order to protect your vocal folds, and if the anesthesiologist knows you're a singer it may be possible to make some accommodations to minimize any chance of discomfort or harm. For example, there are some surgeries that are typically performed with general anesthesia but could instead be accomplished with an epidural or a spinal block. The anesthesiologist may be able to use an anesthetic facemask in lieu of intubation. When intubation is necessary, he or she may be able to utilize a smaller tube and ensure it is inserted as gently as possible.

––––––––––––

It is of paramount importance for you to maintain as healthy a lifestyle as you can, but it is also important that you approach health matters with a spirit of pragmatism rather than paranoia.

- Understanding how your instrument functions will help you discern whether vocal problems stem from technical issues or medical ones.

- Respecting your body as you would an heirloom instrument will motivate you to think of healthy lifestyle habits as a part of your job.

- A strong relationship with a primary care physician will incline you to seek timely medical care when you need it and remove the temptation to self-diagnose and self-medicate.

- Researching and acquiring adequate health insurance will ensure your ability to protect your instrument both at home and on the road.

I'll close this chapter with some final thoughts on supplements: At this point, tinctures and teas are as much a part of classical singer culture as the scarves we layer around our necks whenever the thermometer drops below 68°F. While they may not defend us from illness or speed our recovery as we might wish, they can offer a measure of comfort and reassurance. So I encourage you to continue enjoying your echinacea, licorice, or whatever lemon-honey-ginger-cayenne concoction you swear by. Just understand what it is actually doing for you. Teas and tinctures provide topical warmth, stimulation, and relief—they change the sensations you are experiencing inside your mouth and throat. If your mouth is dry, they might restore a sense of moisture; if your throat is sore, they may provide some subtle numbing of the pain and encourage relaxation of muscles that feel tense from coughing. The herbal remedies you favor can be a vital component of the self-care you engage in to restore you to health, so long as you use them to supplement rather than supplant good overall lifestyle habits and expert medical care.

10

Form Follows Function

Welcome to the age of opera in HD.

Performances are regularly broadcast live to movie theaters all over the world. Opera companies increasingly engage directors with film and theater backgrounds who expect performers to look like the characters they portray. The result has been an escalation in pressure for opera singers to get their bodies into shape for the sake of appearance, with little discussion of the impact it has on their singing.

The opera industry does itself and its singers a terrible disservice when it regards physical appearance and vocal prowess as though they are somehow unrelated. The pressure to slim down or bulk up leads singers to prioritize appearance over the integrity of their instruments and risk engaging in unhealthy diet and exercise strategies. It represents a failure to understand singing as first and foremost a rigorous athletic endeavor.

I frequently hear singers frame questions about fitness in terms of the aesthetic they wish to achieve:

"Can I lose weight without negatively impacting my voice?"

"Can I get six-pack abs without messing up my breathing?"

My response is to point out that form follows function, so a sport-specific fitness regimen designed to optimize singers' bodies for peak performance in singing will likely also yield the aesthetic results they desire. Conversely, a program prioritizing weight loss and/or muscle gain over developing the specialized flexibility, strength, and stability required for excellence in singing can indeed negatively impact the voice.

So ingrained is our culture's emphasis on appearance, however, that I have found it extremely challenging to shift the conversation from one about aesthetics to one about prowess. It seems there is no escaping the conditioning. Even given the breadth of my knowledge and experience in fitness and nutrition, I'd be lying if I said I never felt an urge to pursue a slimmer profile for its own sake.

When I worked full-time as a fitness trainer, one piece of advice that I often received from colleagues and managers went something like this: "Give your clients what they need, but package it in what they say they want." What they meant was that when, as happened with some frequency, a woman approaches me tugging at the underside of her arms and asking, "Can you help me get rid of this?" my response should essentially be "Sure! Here's a routine that will give you firm, shapely arms"—but then I would teach her a comprehensive regimen to improve her overall body composition, hoping that she'll stick with it if I continually point out how each component of her regimen will yield the arms of her dreams.

While the regimen I would design for her actually *is* the means to slimmer arms, my response is not the one she wanted or expected. Nor is it the answer that I instinctively wished to provide.

- *She* wanted one exercise that will tighten and slim a specific body part, in isolation.

- *I* wanted to educate her about how women's bodies tend to store fat in the upper arms and that reducing it requires increasing lean muscle mass throughout the body rather than specifically targeting the arms. *I* wanted her to appreciate that building strength in her chest and back will also strengthen her arms, but that trying to spot-sculpt her triceps without priming the larger muscles of her torso could lead to injury. *I* wanted to motivate her to gain strength, stability, coordination, and grace rather than body-shaming herself about the things she wants to "get rid of." But if I started getting into all of that, she'd probably glaze over before I'd completed a couple of sentences.

While I wrote this book because I want you to regard yourselves as athletes and your bodies as instruments, I am aware that many of you may have picked up a copy because you want to look good in HD. But I'm okay with that, because if you consistently follow the workout and nutrition strategies I've laid out, you will likely succeed in meeting your aesthetic goals while also promoting optimal function of your instrument.

My hope is that, as you draw closer to realizing your aesthetic goals, you will *also* begin to identify as an athlete. That you will exult in your increased energy and strength, just as you take pleasure in the skill and power with which you deploy your voice. That you will head for the gym not just because you want to look your best onstage, but also because you love the way it makes you feel.

I believe that as more singers identify as athletes, we will begin to effect a necessary movement in our industry.

We will educate the greater opera community that there is such a thing as an optimal instrument and that aesthetic concerns must take a backseat to its cultivation. We will promote a broad awareness of what it means to simultaneously be and play an instrument. Objectification will cease because our bodies and our voices will be recognized as one and the same. Our unique appearances will be celebrated rather than measured against irrelevant aesthetic standards.

Our voices and our bodies will serve as radiant examples of form following function.

Glossary

abduction. The action of moving one part of the body farther away from another part. When the vocal folds are separated, as in breathing, they are abducted.

adduction. The action of moving one part of the body closer to another part. When the vocal folds are close together, as in phonation, they are adducted.

agonist. A muscle that contracts to produce a specific movement.

antagonist. A muscle that contracts in opposition to an agonist muscle to counter or decelerate a specific movement.

anterior. Located in the front, either of the entire body or of a specific anatomical structure.

approximation. The action of two objects moving close together. The vocal folds must approximate along their entire length in order to phonate clearly.

arytenoid cartilage. A major cartilage of the larynx. The two arytenoid cartilages are shaped like pointed horns and are attached to the top of the posterior surface of the cricoid cartilage. The arytenoids provide the posterior attachment points for the vocal folds; they are also the connecting point for the muscles that open and close the glottis. See figure 3.1.

basal metabolic rate. A formula for expressing human energy expenditure as the output of calories per square meter of body surface per hour.

Bernoulli principle. A law of physics named for Swiss mathematician and physicist Daniel Bernoulli. The Bernoulli principle is often referenced in vocal pedagogy to explain how air in constant motion produces an air pressure differential below and above the glottis to create the suction that produces periodic vocal fold vibration.

biomechanics. The scientific application of mechanical principles to the human movement system.

bodywork. Any therapeutic modality based on movement, massage, and/or manipulation of the body for the purpose of promoting physical and psychological wellness.

buccinator. A muscle of expression that controls lip movement. The buccinator is located in the wall of the cheek. It draws the cheeks in toward the teeth, assisting with such movements as sucking, whistling, and smiling. See figure 4.11.

cartilage. The firm, flexible connective tissue that comprises the stable structures of the larynx. The laryngeal cartilages gradually ossify (become increasingly more like bone) as the body matures.

cervical. Relating to or located near the seven vertebrae of the spinal column comprising the neck. See figure 1.1.

cilia. Fine, hair-like structures located in the lungs that remove microbes and other debris from the airways.

coccyx. The small triangular bone that forms the very bottom of the spine. The coccyx is commonly called the tailbone. See figure 1.1.

cricoarytenoid. An intrinsic muscle of the larynx. The cricoarytenoid muscles connect the cricoid cartilage to the arytenoid cartilage. The lateral cricoarytenoid muscles adduct the vocal folds; the posterior cricoarytenoid muscles abduct the vocal folds. See figures 3.1 and 3.2.

cricoid cartilage. The cricoid cartilage is one of the principal cartilages that compose the larynx. It is shaped like a signet ring and is located below the thyroid cartilage. See figure 3.5.

cricothyroid muscle. A major muscle of the larynx. The cricothyroid muscles connect the cricoid cartilage to the thyroid cartilage. When engaged, the cricothyroid muscles elongate the vocal folds, modulating pitch and registration. See figure 3.5.

deltoids. A group of muscles located at the top of the shoulder. The deltoids facilitate a variety of movements that lift the arm away from the body. The anterior deltoid flexes and internally rotates the arm; the lateral deltoid abducts the arm, raising it to the side; the posterior deltoid lifts and extends the arm to the back.

depression. A muscular action that moves an anatomical structure into a lower position.

diaphragm. A major muscle of respiration. The diaphragm is a large, dome-shaped muscle that separates the thoracic and abdominal cavities and is the primary muscle of inspiration. The diaphragm is the second-largest muscle of the human body, exceeded only by the gluteus maximus. It is at its greatest point of contraction after a full inhalation. During expiration, the diaphragm returns to a relaxed position. See figure 2.1.

digastric. A muscle that elevates the larynx. The digastric comprises two muscular bellies connected by a tendon that attaches to the hyoid bone; the anterior belly connects to the jaw and the posterior belly to the temporal bone of the skull. See figure 3.7.

elevation. A muscular action that raises an anatomical structure into a higher position.

erector spinae. A group of deep muscles connecting the vertebrae of the spine to one another as well as to the rib cage. They work together to extend the spine. See figure 1.8.

extension. Movement at a joint that increases the angle between the bones intersecting at that joint.

flexion. Movement at a joint that decreases the angle between the bones intersecting at that joint.

gastrocnemius. The largest muscle of the calf. The gastrocnemius facilitates knee flexion and ankle plantar flexion (as in pointing the toe). See figures 1.8 and 1.10.

genioglossus. An extrinsic muscle of the tongue. The genioglossus attaches the tongue to the jaw. It is the muscle that protrudes, or sticks out, the tongue. See figure 4.8.

geniohyoid. A muscle that elevates the larynx. The geniohyoid connects the hyoid bone to the jaw; when it contracts, it moves the hyoid bone forward and up. See figure 3.7.

glottis. The glottis is the space between the unapproximated vocal folds.

gluteal muscles. The muscles that comprise the butt. The gluteus maximus extends the hip to pull the leg back; the gluteus medius and gluteus minimus abduct the hip. See figure 1.8.

hamstrings. A group of muscles located in the posterior thigh. The hamstrings work together to facilitate hip extension, knee flexion and extension, and rotation of the lower leg.

hyoglossus. An extrinsic muscle of the tongue. The hyoglossus attaches the tongue to the hyoid bone. It is the muscle that retracts and depresses the tongue. See figure 4.9.

hyoid bone. The structure from which the larynx is suspended in the throat. The hyoid is a horse-shoe-shaped bone that lies between the chin and the thyroid cartilage. The larynx is suspended from the hyoid bone via the thyrohyoid membrane.

intercostal muscles. The muscles that connect the ribs to one another and comprise the body of the chest wall. The intercostals are significant muscles of respiration, contributing to both inhalation and exhalation. See figure 2.1.

kinematics. The mechanics of movement, viewed independently from the force production that creates movement.

kinesthetic. Relating to the ability to feel and interpret sensations and muscular effort related to movement.

larynx. A complex structure located in the throat that is responsible for vocal vibration. The larynx is often referred to as the voice box. It comprises the cricoid, thyroid, and arytenoid cartilages and houses the vocal folds.

lateral. Located on the side, either of the entire body or of a specific anatomical structure.

latissimus dorsi. The largest muscle of the back. The latissimus dorsi adducts, extends, and internally rotates the arm. It also helps to extend and flex the trunk and assists with both deep inhalation and exhalation. See figure 1.8.

levator scapulae. A muscle that connects the scapula to the cervical vertebrae. It elevates the scapula. See figure 1.6.

levator veli palatini. A muscle that connects the soft palate to the temporal bone. It elevates the soft palate. See figure 4.14.

lumbar. Relating to or located near the five lowest vertebrae of the spinal column. See figure 1.1.

mandible. The bone of the lower jaw.

masseter. The major muscle of the jaw. The masseter muscles raise the lower jaw for chewing and articulation. They connect the mandible to the skull. See figure 4.2.

maxilla. The bones that form the upper jaw. The maxilla are fused to the skull and do not move.

mitochondria. Numerous organelles present in most cells of the human body that are responsible for both cellular respiration and energy production.

mylohyoid. A muscle that elevates the larynx. The mylohyoid attaches the hyoid bone to the jaw; when it contracts, it raises the hyoid bone, tongue, and the floor of the oral cavity. See figure 3.7.

obliques. Major muscles of the abdomen. The internal and external obliques work together to rotate the trunk. See figure 2.8.

omohyoid. A muscle that depresses the larynx. The omohyoid muscles attach the hyoid bone to the scapulae. They depress the larynx and hyoid bone. See figure 3.8.

orbicularis oris. A muscle of expression that controls lip movement. The orbicularis oris encircles the lips and rounds them forward as in puckering. See figure 4.11.

palatoglossus. A muscle that connects the soft palate to the tongue. It elevates the back of the tongue. See figure 4.14.

palatopharyngeus. A muscle that connects the soft palate to the thyroid cartilage. It elevates the larynx. See figure 4.14.

passaggio. A term used by voice teachers to describe pivotal pitch ranges in vocal registration that singers must learn to navigate in order to produce consistent tone quality throughout their vocal range. It is generally agreed that both men and women have two passaggio points, one located between the low and middle range and the other between the middle and high range.

pectoral muscles. Major muscles of the chest. The pectoralis major flexes and adducts the arm; the pectoralis minor stabilizes the scapula and assists with inhalation by raising the ribs. See figure 1.6.

pharynx. The portion of the vocal tract that connects the larynx to the oral and nasal cavities.

phoneme. The smallest phonetic unit of sound in a language.

posterior. Located in the back, either of the entire body or of a specific anatomical structure.

pronation. A foot position or movement causing the weight of the body to be disproportionately placed on the inner edge of the foot, flattening the arches.

quadriceps. A group of muscles located in the anterior thigh. The quadriceps work together to facilitate hip flexion and knee extension.

rectus abdominis. A major muscle of the abdomen, commonly referred to as the "six-pack." The rectus abdominis attaches the pelvis to the rib cage. It flexes the lumbar spine. See figure 2.8.

retraction. A muscular action that draws or pulls an anatomical structure into a farther back position.

rhomboid muscle. A major muscle of the shoulders. The rhomboids connect the scapulae with the thoracic and cervical vertebrae. They retract and rotate the scapulae. See figure 2.9.

sacrum. A large triangular bone at the base of the spine, just above the coccyx. See figure 1.1.

scapulae. The shoulder blades. See figure 2.9.

soleus. A muscle of the calf. The soleus facilitates ankle stability and plantar flexion (as in pointing the toe). See figures 1.8 and 1.10.

sternocleidomastoid. The sternocleidomastoid muscles are the large, strap-like muscles often visible on the sides of the neck. They connect the sternum and clavicle to the mastoid process, which is part of the jaw. See figure 1.6.

sternohyoid. A muscle that depresses the larynx. The sternohyoid attaches the sternum to the hyoid bone. It depresses the hyoid bone. See figure 3.8.

sternothyroid. A muscle that depresses the larynx. The sternohyoid attaches the sternum to the larynx. It depresses the larynx. See figure 3.8.

sternum. The flat bone located in the center of the chest. It provides attachment points for the ribs and is considered part of the rib cage.

stylohyoid. A muscle that elevates the larynx. The stylohyoid connects the hyoid bone to the skull. It elevates the hyoid bone. See figure 3.7.

subglottal. Below the glottis, or vocal folds.

supraglottal. Above the glottis, or vocal folds.

synergist. A muscle that provides secondary assistance for the movement of another.

temporalis. A muscle of the jaw. It connects the jaw to the skull and elevates and retracts the jaw in chewing and articulation. See figure 4.2.

tensor veli palatini. A muscle that connects the soft palate to the skull. It tenses the soft palate. See figure 4.14.

thoracic. Relating to or located near the twelve vertebrae of the spinal column that support the rib cage and thorax. See figure 1.1.

thyroarytenoid muscles. A pair of muscles that form the main body of the vocal folds. The thyroarytenoids stretch from the thyroid cartilage to the arytenoid cartilages. They partner with the cricothyroid muscles to modulate pitch and registration. See figure 3.3.

thyrohyoid. An extrinsic muscle of the larynx. The thyrohyoid connects the hyoid bone to the thyroid cartilage of the larynx. While it is capable of both depressing the hyoid bone and elevating the thyroid cartilage, in singing it functions as a laryngeal depressor. See figure 3.8.

thyroid cartilage. The largest of the laryngeal cartilages. The thyroid cartilage is shaped like a shield and is located in the front of the larynx. See figure 3.5.

tibialis. Muscles connected to the shin, located in the lower leg. The anterior tibialis facilitates dorsiflexion of the ankle (pulling the toe up toward the knee) and inversion of the foot; the posterior tibialis facilitates plantar flexion of the ankle (as in pointing the toe) and inversion of the foot. See figure 1.10.

trachea. The tube that connects the pharynx and larynx to the lungs. The trachea is commonly called the windpipe.

transversus abdominis. A major muscle of the abdomen. The muscle fibers of the transversus abdominis are arranged horizontally across the viscera; its action is to compress the contents of the abdomen in order to stabilize the spine. See figure 2.8.

trapezius. A muscle of the shoulders and back that moves the scapulae and arms. The upper portion of the trapezius elevates the shoulders; the middle and lower portions of the trapezius work in tandem with the rhomboids to retract and depress the scapulae. See figure 2.9.

viscera. The organs and other anatomical structures located within the abdominal cavity.

vocal folds. A paired system of tissue layers in the larynx that vibrate to produce phonation. The vocal folds are often referred to as the vocal cords. See figure 3.2.

zygomaticus major. A muscle of expression that controls lip movement. The zygomaticus major draws the lips up and to the sides, as in smiling. See figure 4.11.

Additional Resources

Working Out at Home or on the Road

Minimal equipment is required to perform the exercises in chapter 6, and you can pack light-weight portable versions when traveling. Here is a list of essentials.

Exercise mat. Hard floors and carpets can be slippery or uneven. Use a mat when exercising away from the gym for both prone and upright movements. Take a slim, lightweight mat (under 2 pounds) with you on the road.

Resistance bands with handles and door anchors. Rubber resistance bands provide a wide range of tension and challenge and can substitute for both cable machines and dumbbells. Pack a pair in light- and medium-weight resistance when traveling.

Dumbbells. The exercises in chapter 6 are designed to be performed with light- to medium-weight dumbbells, so a small selection ranging from 3 pounds to 12 pounds is all you need at home. Travel dumbbells are available that weigh less than 2 pounds per pair and can be filled with water to weigh up to 16 pounds each.

Foam roller. Foam rollers are available in varying degrees of firmness, so choose one that meets your comfort level. Collapsible versions are available for travel.

Personal massager. A large, durable massager is helpful, not only for addressing post-exercise tension but also for alleviating the muscular kinks that accumulate from long flights or sleeping in unfamiliar beds.

Stable exercise shoes. Cross trainers are best for strength training exercises. Choose a shoe that provides your feet and legs with solid support. The stabilization exercises in chapter 6 will be safer and more effective when you are not also required to compensate for unstable footwear.

Anatomy

Bozeman, Kenneth. *Practical Vocal Acoustics: Pedagogic Applications for Teachers and Singers.* Hillsdale, NY: Pendragon Press, 2014.

Kenneth Bozeman's book makes vocal acoustics accessible and easily applicable in the studio. This is a concise, practical guide for understanding and improving the way singers define vowels, amplify vocal production, and vary timbre.

Calais-Germain, Blandine. *Anatomy of Movement*. Seattle: Eastland Press, 1993.

Calais-Germain, Blandine. *Anatomy of Breathing*. Seattle: Eastland Press, 2006.

Calais-Germain, Blandine and François Germain. *Anatomy of Voice*. New York: Healing Arts Press, 2016.

Blandine Calais-Germain's anatomy series features beautiful, detailed illustrations by the author, as well as accessible descriptions. *Anatomy of Movement* is widely used as a textbook for dance curricula. I frequently refer to *Anatomy of Breathing* and *Anatomy of Voice* in the studio and found them highly valuable in researching this book.

Kapit, Wynn, and Lawrence M. Elson. *The Anatomy Coloring Book*. New York: Pearson, 2013.

If you are a more visual than conceptual learner, you may find coloring the illustrations in this book far less intimidating than reading an anatomy text. Choose a color for each anatomical structure shown in an image; then color in its name, read the description, and color in the structure. If you prefer, focus on only those sections relevant to vocal anatomy.

Malde, Melissa. "Mapping the Structures of Resonance," *Journal of Singing* 65:4 (March–April 2009).

Melissa Malde is a voice teacher and body mapping specialist. This article provides clear, concise descriptions of the articulators and highlights the distinctions between objective anatomical function and the way singers often subjectively experience the movements of articulation.

McCoy, Scott Jeffrey. *Your Voice: An Inside View*. Princeton, NJ: Inside View Press, 2004.

Scott McCoy's classic pedagogy and vocology textbook features not only a comprehensive array of anatomical illustrations but also a wealth of interactive video and audio examples.

Sinav, Ahmet, MD. *The Larynx*. https://www1.columbia.edu/sec/itc/hs/medical/anatomy_resources/anatomy/larynx/ College of Physicians and Surgeons, Columbia University, 2005.

This interactive atlas of laryngeal anatomy includes labeled illustrations of different views of the larynx, animations of intrinsic laryngeal muscle activity, and video footage of human movement.

Vibrant Voice Technique. https://www.vibrantvoicetechnique.com.

Vibrant Voice Technique is a system for using handheld massagers to alleviate the muscular tension that can cause vocal fatigue, as well as enhance breathing, resonance, and range. The massage techniques recommended in chapters 3 and 4 are drawn from this method. External vibration provides an effective means of releasing the small muscles governing laryngeal function and articulation in much the same way that self-myofascial release techniques prepare larger muscle groups in accordance with corrective exercise protocols.

Wolf, Jessica. *Jessica Wolf's Art of Breathing* [DVD]. http://www.jessicawolfartofbreathing.com/rib-animation/ 2013.

Jessica Wolf is an Alexander teacher who specializes in breathing rehabilitation. Her *Art of Breathing* DVD is a three-dimensional narrated animation of breathing that begins with the bare skeletal system and progresses through increasingly complex layers of musculature. It offers a thorough visual representation of the anatomy and movements involved in breathing.

The Mind/Body Connection

Feldenkreis, Moshe. *Awareness Through Movement: Easy-to-Do Health Exercises to Improve Your Posture, Vision, Imagination, and Personal Awareness*. San Francisco: HarperOne, 2009.

This is the classic introductory text for the Feldenkreis Method, written by its creator.

Gelb, Michael J. *Body Learning: An Introduction to the Alexander Technique*. New York: Henry Holt, 1996.

This book provides a solid introduction to the history and methodology of the Alexander Technique.

Malde, Melissa, MaryJean Allen, and Kurt-Alexander Zeller. *What Every Singer Needs to Know About the Body*. San Diego: Plural Publishing, 2016.

This book applies principles of body mapping to vocal anatomy and singing technique. Discussions of anatomy and movement are accompanied by exercises for improving kinesthetic awareness and function.

Salzberg, Sharon, and Joseph Goldstein. *Insight Meditation: A Step-by-Step Course on How to Meditate*. Louisville, CO: Sounds True, 2002.

This self-study course is a thorough introduction to insight meditation created by two prominent clinicians who are skilled at teaching mindfulness techniques without any trappings of religiosity. It includes two CDs of guided meditations.

Thompson, Cathy, and Tara Thompson. *The Thompson Method of Bodywork: Structural Alignment, Core Strength, and Emotional Release*. New York: Healing Arts Press, 2018.

Cathy and Tara Thompson's book is a comprehensive road map for mind/body integration and tension release. Their bodywork clientele consists largely of performing artists, including classical singers and voice teachers.

Fitness

Manocchia, Pat. *Anatomy of Exercise: A Trainer's Inside Guide to Your Workout*. Richmond Hill, ON: Firefly Books, 2009.

This guide to strength training exercises provides detailed descriptions of the musculature and biomechanics involved in each movement.

National Academy of Sports Medicine. YouTube Channel. https://www.youtube.com/user/NASMorg/videos. Blog http://blog.nasm.org/

NASM's YouTube channel offers an expanding collection of instructional exercise videos; you will find videos corresponding to most of the stretches and exercises described in this book. The "Quick Fix: Arms Fall Forward" video (https://youtu.be/qMOc_xXjKa8) lays out an effective corrective exercise sequence for upper crossed syndrome (figure 1.7). Their blog includes numerous posts describing corrective exercise protocols for specific muscular imbalances. http://blog.nasm.org/category/ces/. While NASM's online content is directed at fitness trainers, the information they provide is valuable for anyone who wishes to make their exercise regimen safer and more effective.

Page, Phillip, Clare Frank, and Robert Lardner. *Assessment and Treatment of Muscle Imbalance: The Janda Approach*. Champaign, IL: Human Kinetics, 2009.

This book offers a detailed account of Vladimir Janda's approach to postural assessment and expands on his techniques for alleviating distortions and imbalances.

Nutrition

Benardot, Dan. *Advanced Sports Nutrition*. Champaign, IL: Human Kinetics, 2011.

This popular sports nutrition textbook offers strategies to fuel your body for training, recovery, and peak performance in any physical endeavor. While Benardot's coverage of such topics as the science of metabolism and chemistry of various nutrients may be more in-depth than is useful for the layman, his philosophy on diet and body composition will encourage you to view food as fuel and bodyweight as a component of how your instrument functions.

Harris-Benedict BMR Calculator. https://manytools.org/handy/bmr-calculator/.

This version of the Harris-Benedict calculator factors in your overall activity level and will therefore yield a more accurate result.

US Department of Health and Human Services. *Dietary Guidelines for Americans 20152020*. https://health.gov/dietaryguidelines/2015/resources/2015-2020_Dietary_Guidelines.pdf.

This book is available as a free download. It contains all of the fundamental information you need to construct a balanced, nutritious meal plan. When you consider the staggering proliferation of marketing campaigns to promote hyperpalatable foods and fad diets, it may come as a surprise that these publicly funded, well-researched guidelines are available for free. Tune out the ads and teach yourself to eat well.

Health and Medicine

Sataloff, Robert T. *Vocal Health and Pedagogy: Science, Assessment, and Treatment*. San Diego: Plural Publishing, 2017.

Robert Sataloff is a leading otolaryngologist and a prominent member of the vocal health community. His book is an essential primer on maintaining vocal health, troubleshooting dysfunctions, and seeking appropriate medical interventions as needed.

US Department of Health and Human Services Prevention and Wellness Resources. https://www.hhs.gov/programs/prevention-and-wellness/index.html.

This site is a portal for accessing a variety of health and medical resources, including disease prevention, lifestyle recommendations, and mental health support.

Index

inhalation, 26, 27; breath as generator, 23–35; cycle, 29; diaphragm and, xvii, xviii, 3, *24–27*, 24–28, 162; during exercise, 85–86; exercises for coordination, 35–38; health issues, 151–52, 154; lung tissue, 28, 31; meditation and, 80–81; onsets and releases, 37; scapular retraction exercise, 28; schools of, 33; stage movement and, xv, 22; stamina and, xv; subglottal breath pressure, xv, xvii, 23, 31–34, 48, 165; supraglottal tract, xvii; survival, comfort, and expression, 23; thoracic spine and, 3; "turn your breath around" exercise, 27, 29, 36–38; unconscious holding, 28; upper crossed syndrome, 6; voluntary and involuntary, 25; warming up, 136; without vocalizing, 37

buccinator, 67, *67*, 68, *68*, *69*, 70, 161

Bunch, Meribeth, ix

calves, 18; calf raises, 120; SMR for, 90, *90*; static stretch, 98, *98*

canceling performance, 157

carbohydrates, 142

cardiopulmonary rescucitation (CPR), 34

cardiorespiratory fitness, xv, xvii, 34–35, 38, 132–33; interval training, 35, 132

cartilage, 162

Caruso, Enrico, ix

cervical flexors, *50*, *51*

cervical spine, 2, *2*, 3, 48; alignment, 50–52, *51*

Cher, vii

chest, sensations in, xvii, 26. *See* core; torso

chest presses, 108, *109–12*, 113

"chest voice," 52

chin, alignment, 15

cilia, 152

clarinet example, vii, xix, 149

Classical Singer Magazine, ix

classical singers, acoustic, xx, 1–2

conduction, xvii, 77

connective tissue, 86

consistency, xvi, 23

coordination, xvii, 35–38

core, xv, 18; lower crossed syndrome, 7, *9*; multi-planar balance/reach, 120, *121–23*; planks, 120, *124*, 125, *125*; single leg scaption, 113, *114–15*; strength and stabilization training, 101, 120, *124–25*, 126–32; strength challenge, 125. *See also* obliques; torso

corrective exercise protocols, 21–22

coughing, 151, 155

cricoarytenoid muscles, 40, *40*, *41*

cricoid cartilage, 44, 162

cricothyroid joints, 46

cricothyroid muscles, 6, 42, *43*, *44*, 44–45, 52, 53, 162

curtsy squat, 116

deltoids, 18, 162; single leg scaption, 113

depressors, 45, *45*, *46*, 48, 162

diaphragm, xvii, 3, *24–27*, 24–28, 162; "sing/engage (from)," xviii, 28

diarrhea, 157

diet industry, 146, 147

digastric muscle, 45, *46*, 49, *50*, 162

door anchor, 108, 113, 129, 167

Doscher, Barbara, ix

dumbbells, 113, 116, *117*, 167

dysfunction, xvii–xviii, 12; imbalances, xviii–xix. *See also* lower crossed syndrome; pronation distortion syndrome; tensions; upper crossed syndrome

ear, 77

eating disorders, 146

elevators, 45, *45*, *46*, 48, 162

equanimity, 79–80, 81

erector spinae, 18, 162

études, 137

exercise mat, 167

extension, 162

feet, alignment, *13*, 15

Feldenkrais, Moshe, 83

Feldenkrais Method, 83

fever, 155, 157

financial issues, 150

fitness certification programs, 148

flexion, 163

foam roller, 86, 167

focus and concentration, 79–81, 137–38

Food and Drug Administration (FDA), 141, 151

force production, xiv, 45, 163

form follows function, xiii, 159–60

gastrocnemius, 163; static stretch, 98, *98*

gastroesophageal reflux (GERD), 154, 155

Gelb, Peter, 149

generator, xvi–xvii; breath as, 23–35; warm up, 137. *See also* breathing

genioglossus, 63, *63*, 64, *64*, *65*, 67, 163

geniohyoid muscle, 163

glossopalatine, 72

About the Author

Claudia Friedlander, DMUS, NASM-CPT, CES, PES, is a voice teacher and fitness expert based in New York City. Born in Queens and raised in New Jersey, she began her musical studies as a clarinetist. Her passion was fueled by her early experiences playing in the Young Artists Orchestra at Tanglewood under the batons of Seiji Ozawa and Leonard Bernstein. This led to private studies with Richard Stoltzman, a master's degree in clarinet from Peabody Conservatory, and a brief stint as the principal clarinetist of Orquesta Sinfónica del Estado de México.

Shortly after completing her undergraduate studies at Bennington College, she was encouraged to study singing by conductor Blanche Honegger Moyse. She sang while continuing to play her instrument, earning a master's degree in voice at Peabody. Eventually, her fascination with the physiological process of singing eclipsed her passion for clarinet. In 1995, she began doctoral studies in vocal performance and pedagogy at McGill University, which she completed in 1999.

In 2002, Dr. Friedlander moved to New York City, apprenticed herself to renowned pedagogue W. Stephen Smith, and established her voice studio. In her first few years of teaching, frustration with her inability to methodically and rigorously address the mechanical dysfunctions of some of her students motivated her to study kinesiology. After receiving her certification as a personal trainer from the National Academy of Sports Medicine, she became inspired to apply the concept of sports-specific training to professional voice training.

Dr. Friedlander has presented workshops on vocal fitness for the Voice Foundation and the Performing Arts Medicine Association and was an invited panel discussant on health and wellness for Opera America. Her students have performed on Broadway and at leading opera houses including the Santa Fe Opera and the Metropolitan Opera. She is the author of the monthly column "Musings on Mechanics" for *Classical Singer* magazine, as well as writing a widely read and cited blog on vocal technique and fitness, *The Liberated Voice*. In 2008 she joined the faculty of the Weill Music Institute at Carnegie Hall, where her most recent project was the development, in collaboration with Joyce DiDonato, of *The Singer's Audition Handbook*, an interactive online career development guide for young singers.

About the Artists

Artist and occupational therapist **Sandy Escobar**'s diverse projects include anatomical illustration, community art, mental health support, and health-care research. She has been creating art for ten years and has previously illustrated vocal anatomy for publications and web content for the Vibrant Voice Technique. Sandy is passionate about creating accessible, inclusive spaces in health care, communities, and people's homes. Her broad-ranging activities include producing collaborative murals, holding workshops to design accessible spaces for people with mental illnesses, and recommending orthopaedic equipment to clients. She earned a BFA in interdisciplinary visual art from the Nova Scotia College of Art and Design, and MS in occupational therapy from Dalhousie University.

Photographer **Daniel Welch** combines his artistic, technical, acting, and musical training to create dynamic images for books, magazines, billboards, and album covers. While Daniel's subjects include performers of all types, his work reflects his enduring passion for classical singing. He is artistic director of Reclamation Opera, a company that produces film versions of operatic masterpieces designed to delight new audiences and offer fresh perspectives to die-hard fans.

Soprano **Kirsten Chambers** has performed with the Metropolitan Opera, Florida Grand Opera, and New York City Opera and has appeared in concert with the American Symphony Orchestra and The Orchestra Now. Her signature roles are among the most physically demanding in the repertoire and include the title role in *Salome* and Elsa in *Lohengrin*. While fitness had been an important part of Kirsten's life growing up, exercise eventually took a backseat to her musical studies. She soon got a wake-up call: "One day I was in a staging rehearsal that required my character to run up and down stairs and then sing long declaratory phrases. . . . I kept running out of breath!" She took up a regimen that includes cardio and strength training and now has stamina to burn. Kirsten finds that fitness supports her singing in many ways: "I move more naturally on stage; my voice warms up faster and more efficiently; mentally, I'm more focused; and the improvements to my posture have stabilized my breath."

Baritone **David Adam Moore** has performed with major opera companies worldwide, including the Metropolitan Opera, Teatro alla Scala, Covent Garden, Lyric Opera of Chicago, and the Salzburg Festival. A celebrated interpreter of contemporary music, he has created roles for some of today's most important living composers, including Thomas Adès, Peter Eötvös, and David T. Little. He is also known for his work as a stage director, composer, and video designer, frequently collaborating on multimedia productions of both classic and new works. While on the road, David enjoys parkour as a means of both challenging himself physically and becoming acquainted with new cities. He experiences his artistry and physicality as deeply integrated but emphasizes the primacy of vocal excellence for opera performance: "A full, beautiful voice and an engaging character will always give audiences more goose bumps than well-defined abs."